LEARNING HOW TO LEARN

Getting Into and Surviving College When You Have a Learning Disability

JOYANNE COBB

CWLA PRESS ■ WASHINGTON, DC

CHILD WELFARE LEAGUE OF AMERICA, INC.
HEADQUARTERS
440 First Street, NW, Third Floor, Washington, DC 20001-2085
E-mail: books@cwla.org

CURRENT PRINTING (last digit)
10 9 8 7 6 5 4 3 2 1

Cover design by James D. Melvin
Text design by Pen & Palette

Printed in the United States of America
ISBN # 0–87868–776–9

Library of Congress Cataloging-in-Publication Data
Cobb, Joyanne.
    Learning how to learn: getting into and surviving college when you have a learning disability / by Joyanne Cobb.
        p. cm.
    Includes bibliographical references.
    ISBN 0-87868-776-9

    1. Learning diabled–Education (Higher)–United States. 2. Universities and colleges–United States–Admission. I. Title.

LC4818.38 .C762 2001

371.92'6–dc21

99-045582

TABLE OF CONTENTS

ACKNOWLEDGMENTS

This book would not have been possible without the help of many people who have been there for me when times were very rough and I didn't know if I was going to achieve my goals.

First and foremost, I would like to express my deepest gratitude to Barbara Seaman, a now-retired English professor, without whom this book would not have happened. She not only helped me develop the overall vision of this book, but devoted hours of assistance with the research, editing, and revisions. More than that, she believed in me when I did not believe in myself, made me fight the system and appeal a graduate school entrance decision, and was a mother to me in so many ways. Her support and inspiration has and always will carry me through tough times.

Cathy Corder came to my rescue as a tutor in college and then realized I had a wealth of information that I should share with the world in the form of this book. I will never forget her tireless hours of work with me.

Christy Willis of the George Washington University was a savior to me and many other disabled students at the Disabled Student Services Office. She is still there today.

Erica Lovelace of the Virginia Department of Rehabilitative Services implemented a great plan for me.

Other people that would not give up on me and gave me strength when I thought that I had none were Barbara Wagner and family, Betty Wright, Laura Martin, Candice Merkle, Lisa Courtney, Diane Nichols, Vicki Dorn-Fontana, Annette Carapellucci, and Barbara Berhmann. I cannot thank you all enough.

A special thanks goes to my family, my partner Margaret, and my many friends. You put up with a lot, as I know at times I have not been the easiest person to deal with.

And finally a big thank you goes to the Child Welfare League of America for taking a chance on an unknown author, and particularly to Tegan Culler for her thoughtful editing. Your efforts here will make a difference for many learning disabled persons.

INTRODUCTION: THE INVISIBLE DISABILITY

So you want to go to college—but you have a learning disability. I also struggled through high school with a learning disability, and my counselors were convinced that I should just prepare for a career at some fast-food outlet. But I decided that I deserved better. I got into college and got my undergraduate degree. I finished graduate school and earned a master's degree—and I also learned a lot about how learning disabled students like you and me can succeed in college.

If you are learning disabled, you are a person who learns differently. Sure, you have a disability, in the sense that you receive and process information differently—so that you can't learn in the traditional ways that your peers do. You may have visual sequencing problems that cause you to have trouble seeing things in correct order. You may have visual discrimination problems and can't see the difference between two similar objects, letters, or numbers. Or maybe you have a form of a processing disorder called dyslexia, which causes you to see letters, syllables, words, and even numbers reversed or just out of order. Speech and language disorders are another form of a learning disability. Articulation disorder, which affects your ability to control speech rate; expressive language disorder, which is a problem expressing yourself in speech; and receptive language disorder, which is trouble understanding certain aspects of speech.

These are just some of the reasons why you learn differently, and that puts you at a disadvantage. When you start the race 50 yards behind the other runners, you can't be expected to finish at the same time everyone else does.

One of the most painful things about having a learning disability is that it is very difficult for people to understand. Just as with racism and bigotry, that which we do not understand we treat differently—and sometimes with more than a little animosity. I believe this lack of understanding is the most difficult thing for people with learning disabilities and for their families to deal with.

I never realized how painful this invisible disability was for me until one night in October 1990. I had been asked to participate on a panel during Disability Awareness Week at George Washington University, where I was an undergraduate. On the panel were other people with various disabilities. A male student and I represented the learning disabled population.

The format was for each person on the panel to tell our "stories," followed by a question-and-answer period. I was doing fine until someone in the audience asked me, "What is the hardest thing about having a disability that you cannot see? I can see that she is in a wheelchair and he is blind, but how do people react to someone who looks fine but claims to be disabled? I mean, you look fine to me."

For a long time there was silence. I remember staring at the sign language interpreter as she waited patiently for me to respond. At that point, I could feel the tears welling up in my eyes and my face starting to burn. I began to say, "You know, it is so hard to ask for help when people think that you don't need it or don't understand why you need it," but I couldn't get all this out in one fell swoop. I began to cry. I kept saying, "Wait a minute," as I tried to collect myself and muster what little dignity I had left to finish what I was trying to say. To tell you the truth, I don't remember if I ever got the whole statement out, but I think about 70 people understood something about a learning disability that night.

Going to college may be more difficult for someone who is learning disabled, but I know from experience that it can be done. Your decision to go to college is the right one, because it is what you want to do, and that is all the justification you need.

This guide is designed to help you reach your goals. In a nutshell, this book will address

✎ knowing your rights under the Americans with Disabilities Act of 1990 (ADA);

✎ preparing for college by thinking about issues and concerns in high school;

✎ getting the proper documentation of your learning disability to ensure you get services you need;

✎ taking the SAT and the ACT;

✎ researching schools with services for the learning disabled;

✎ asking the questions that will help you choose the college or university that is right for you;

✎ making your college life easier with assistive technology (computer programs and other instruments);

✎ and adapting my own tips for getting into and surviving college with a learning disability.

Along the way I have shared my own experiences, so you can understand the challenges you will be meeting. I hope you will find some useful suggestions in the stories I have to tell.

You need to know that you can go to college and succeed. I am proof of that, though I made several mistakes along the way. My hope is that this guide will help you avoid making the same ones that I did, and you may be able to get your bachelor's degree in four or five years—instead of seven years, like me. But do keep in mind that although it may take you longer than other people, **it can be done!**

CHAPTER 1:

THE AMERICANS WITH DISABILITIES ACT

Having a learning disability means, quite simply, that you have a disability. Educators, psychological professionals, medical professionals, and even learning disabled persons such as you often do not make this connection. This missed connection many times is why persons with learning disabilities do not access and utilize the legislation that is put in place to protect their right to reasonable accommodations.

All civil rights laws that concern persons with disabilities, from the Rehabilitation Act of 1973 to the Americans with Disabilities Act of 1990, do recognize individuals with learning disabilities. This means that you are entitled to the same unique civil rights protections given to persons with other types of disabilities. Your coverage under this Act is relevant to your college education.

Under the ADA, the term disability means a physical or mental impairment that substantially limits a person in a major life activity. Persons with a learning disability are covered here because a major life function, (i.e., learning) is substantially limited or impaired. However, in an educational setting you must be up to at least the standards of the program you are entering. The law states that a qualified individual with a disability is someone who with or without reasonable accommodations can meet the criteria for entry into the educational program. Although they are required to provide "reasonable accommodation" for your disability once you are admitted, the college does not have to change its educational standards for admittance in order to accommodate you. You must first meet their criteria for admittance before gaining access to these civil rights.

Professional documentation of the learning disability is required prior to the provision of the accommodations. It will be up to you to disclose your disability and when. Disability laws forbid employers or educational institutions from asking as part of their interview process if a person has a disability. This means it is up to you to self-disclose in order to be guaranteed protection under the law. Do not wait to disclose after you are in trouble in a class. It creates even more stress and may be too late to help you.

Under the ADA, "reasonable accommodation" may include auxiliary aids and services a learning disabled person may require. Auxiliary aides and services include qualified interpreters or other effective methods of making aurally delivered materials available, qualified readers, taped texts, acquisition or modified equipment or devices, and other similar services and actions. These "reasonable accommodations" are the things that allow you as a student to achieve your goals.

An essential part of your success is your ability to advocate for yourself. Not that you should set up picket lines and start a coalition, but you should learn how to ask for what you need. Keep in mind that it is **your right** to be accommodated. However, if you don't ask for those accommodations, you won't get them. As I have already mentioned, learning disabilities are invisible. That means that the average Joe is not going to be able to see what you need.

To advocate for yourself means to speak up and speak to the right people. If your professors are not familiar with learning disabilities, then use the opportunity to educate them. Talk about your experiences with LD peers in your support and resources groups. You are your own greatest advocate, and just as you have had to learn how to learn, you will have to self-advocate to survive in college.

Some people think that the "LD" should stand for "Learning Differently," not "Learning Disabled." You're right to refer to yourself as someone who learns differently. But if we only say that we are people who learn **differently,** then we are also saying that we are not **disabled**. In that case, legislation on accommodations for the disabled would no longer apply to us. Consequently, when you describe yourself as someone who learns differently, you're perfectly right. But when you are fighting for accommodations in a traditional academic arena, you should refer to yourself as "learning disabled."

Finally, know the law. Understanding the ADA is important because it entitles you to the accommodations that you deserve. Here are some toll-free numbers you can use to find out about what the law provides for a person with a learning disability:

✎ **The ADA Information Line** (800-514-0301/voice and 800-514-0383/ TDD) can answer your questions about the law, send you free material, and advise you on how to file an **ADA** complaint.

✎ **The ADA Information Center for the Mid-Atlantic region** (800-949-4232) can provide you with the same general information.

✎ **Department of Justice Information Line** (800-514-0301) can give you information about the **Rehabilitation Act (Section 504),** another law that protects your rights, and can advise you about filing a complaint on violations other than educational ones.

✎ **Department of Education, Office of Civil Rights** (1-800-421-3481) not only answers questions about **Section 504** but also provides advice on how to file a **Section 504** complaint on education-related issues.

To make the law work for you, however, you must be able to document your disability and know what accommodations you need. Find out about your legal rights; they are an essential part of your educational plan.

PART ONE

GETTING INTO COLLEGE

Classroom 101

CHAPTER 2:
PREPARING FOR COLLEGE

I cannot emphasize enough that this journey you are embarking on, this path of higher education, will be a constant process of learning how to learn. For you to accomplish your goal—going to college—you will need to make many preparations. It's a process that should begin when you start high school. It is a long process, but with the right planning and assistance, you can do it.

Let me begin by telling you just a little about my experience in high school, before I even started thinking about going to college. At that time, I didn't think that I had the ability to make my own decisions about anything related to school. I was led to believe that I was lacking something, and therefore, deciding what classes I was going to take was something that I couldn't possibly do right.

I had a counselor who saw that I could not succeed in the classroom (my grades were proof of that), so I was signed up for classes like "Leadership," which was an invaluable experience and probably helped my self-esteem somewhat. But I was registered for a lot of study hall, too. Because I failed most of the science and math courses I took, I had little to show that I could succeed in the classroom—that I could learn.

I had done a science project in which I designed my own methods to present a problem and conducted experiments to examine that problem. My project was on acid rain, and I presented it to the International Science and Engineering Fair for four consecutive years. I did it at my own pace and was able to present it orally in competitions, instead of on paper or in an exam format. This option was ideal for me, as someone who learns differently, since I could not pass a chemistry class to save my life and did a mediocre job in biology courses.

Although I felt confident about my project, after I returned to the classroom I was unable to comprehend the same information I had used in my experiment, because I didn't understand the way it was presented. While other students with good science projects were being offered scholarships to colleges, I was left behind with a great project but failing grades. When other students would ask me where I was going to college, I wanted so much to be like them that I would lie and say, "Oh, I got offers, too, but I don't know where I'll be going."

Then, the summer before my senior year in high school, I was given a scholarship to a summer college science program, with the option of attending that college after graduation. There I worked with a college professor on my research and science project, did well, and was even chosen to return the next year and present it at a junior science symposium. But another part of that program was to take classes—and pass them. Again, the roadblocks went up. Of all the students who made presentations, I was the only one with no plans to attend college after graduation. I struggled with this bleak prospect for a long time. Many people would see me with my science project and then expect me to reproduce it successfully on paper or in the classroom. They just automatically thought that I'd be going to a great college or university and have all my ducks in a row. But the truth was my ducks were drowning and I really did not have a plan to save them.

I started my uphill battle at the University of Florida by failing those classes, then going to a community college in my hometown and failing there. I dealt with all this failure by making bad choices about drugs and alcohol but, through it all, I knew I had to figure out what I needed to reach the potential I knew I had. I had to **learn how to learn** all over again. With each failure and each school I learned something. It took me seven years to get my bachelor's degree, but I did it. Along the way I found out more and more things that would make learning easier for me. Eventually I found a community college that provided an environment that allowed me to learn and then I transferred to one of the best universities in the country with superb services to learning-disabled students, George Washington University. I hope that this book and the account of my journey makes yours an easier one.

SCHEDULING: THE FIRST STEP

So how can you avoid similar roadblocks? The first important step you should take to prepare for college is to have a "hands-on" experience with your high school class schedule. You should allow your counselor to help, but you must know your own capabilities, too. You probably have had to "learn how to learn" all your life, so your input into deciding which classes to take will be invaluable as you journey toward your college degree.

As I said before, you know what you can do, so you are the best judge of the workload you can carry each semester. You should certainly take some courses in subjects that you will enjoy, but don't let a counselor or a teacher tell you that these are the **only** ones that you can do well in. And when you are making your schedule, be sure to consider participation in extracurricular activities.

My Experience: I did well in extracurricular activities, but I didn't have good grades. Then, too, my time management skills were poor. Because I succeeded in activities outside the classroom, I wanted to do more of them. As a result, I spent so little time on the classwork that I failed miserably. On the other hand, my success in extracurricular activities gave me good memories of high school. I did well on the tennis court, in a speech tournament, and on the stage. Without these activities, I probably would have felt like a complete failure and may not have had the little confidence I did. I recommend participation in extracurricular activities, but participate with caution. Limit yourself. Be sure to make the extra time you need to put into that difficult class. You need to feel success and accomplishment outside the classroom, but don't overdo it to the point that you jeopardize your success in the classroom.

INDIVIDUAL EDUCATION PLAN

Some of you may have had the opportunity to make choices for yourself in the writing of your Individual Education Plan. Although student involvement in IEPs is now a recommended policy, it may not occur regularly in all schools. I was not involved in this process and did not know that I should have been. Had I been involved, I could have taken a first step toward self-empowerment, and perhaps my journey through college wouldn't have been such a long one. So my advice is to be involved in this process. It is the best for you in the long run, as it will help you to realize your challenges and strengths.

FOREIGN LANGUAGES

For many learning disabled people, learning a foreign language is a major roadblock. Since this is a requirement in many high schools and colleges, learning disabled students face a seemingly insurmountable barrier. Therefore, scheduling a foreign language course is something to consider carefully. Begin by finding out if your high school requires a foreign language for graduation and whether the colleges you are considering require it.

As a learning disabled person, you need to consider many factors in your decision to study a foreign language: the instructor, the pace at which the class is taught, and the experiences you have had with studying a foreign language, if any. If you have had difficulty with one language, try a new one. You will be more likely to succeed with a language that uses an alphabet with which you are familiar. In addition to these considerations, you should also find out about your peers in the course. If most of the other students have no experience in this language, you may find yourself (maybe for the first time) at the same starting point as other students.

My Experience: My first attempt to learn a foreign language was with Spanish. I started out well enough, but only seemed to get worse as the class moved on, and I began to repeat my frustrating experiences trying to learn to write in English. The next disaster was Latin. (Yes, I even flunked Latin.) That experience was particularly frustrating, because I had a very difficult time understanding the differences between words, whether I heard them or read them. It's no surprise that when I had the chance, I opted to take a foreign culture course in college.

Some teachers of foreign languages are reassessing their thinking about dyslexic learners, and some may be able to modify their courses to accommodate your needs. For example, many people with learning disabilities can learn a foreign language auditorily by using cassette tapes or by using a computer program that allows them to learn by visual cues. A software program, Climbing with Phonics, is now available for those with "phonemic awareness" problems.

If your learning disability prevents you from learning a foreign language, however, check to see if you have the option to take a foreign culture course or if you can substitute any other class. Finally, if you have no other option, find out if you can have the foreign language requirement waived. A list of publications and electronic sources on learning disabilities and foreign languages appears at the end of this chapter.

To sum up, some of the obstacles you may encounter in preparing for college involve becoming involved in your class scheduling, including courses that may be required by colleges or universities, and taking foreign languages. With a little planning and some work, however, you **can** meet these challenges.

PRINT RESOURCES ON LEARNING DISABILITIES AND ADD/ADHD

Bell, N. (1991). Visualizing and verbalizing (2nd ed.). Paso Robles, CA: Academy of Reading Publications.

Clark, D.B. & Uhrey, J.K. (1995). <u>Dyslexia: Theory & practice of remedial instruction</u>. (2nd ed.). Baltimore: York Press.

The Coordinated Campaign for Learning Disabilities. (1997). <u>Commonly asked questions about learning disabilities</u>. Online: http://www. ldonline.org/

Dartmouth College. (1997). <u>Academic success video series for college students</u>. Online: http:/www.dartmouth.edu/admin/acskills/

Franklin, L., Hodge, M.E., & Sasscer, M.F. (1997). Improving retention with strategy-based instruction. <u>The Journal of the Virginia Community Colleges, 1</u>(2).

PRINT RESOURCES ON LEARNING DISABILITIES AND FOREIGN LANGUAGES

Bacon, S.M. (1996). Choices in postsecondary foreign language programs. In B. H.Wing (Ed.), <u>Foreign languages for all: Challenges and choices</u> (pp. 91–114). Lincolnwood, IL: National Textbook Company.

Otto, S. K. & Pusak, J. P. (1996). Technological choices to meet the challenges. In B. H. Wing (Ed.), <u>Foreign languages for all: Challenges and choices</u> (pp. 141–186). Lincolnwood, IL: National Textbook Company.

Schwartz, R. L. (1997). <u>Learning disabilities and foreign language learning: A painful collision</u>. Online: http://www.ldonline.org/ld_indepth/foreign_lang/painful_collision.html.

Sedita, J. (1996). <u>A call for more study skills: Instruction</u>. Online: http://www.ldonline.org/

Sparks, R. & Ganschow, L. (1993). The impact of native language learning problems on foreign language learning: Case study illustrations of the linguistic coding deficit hypothesis. <u>The Modern Language Journal, 77</u>, 58–74.

Sparks, R., Ganschow, L., Pohlman, J., Skinner, S., & Artzer, M. (1992). The effect of multisensory structured language instruction on native language and foreign language aptitude skills of at-risk foreign language learners. <u>Annals of Dyslexia, 42</u>, 25–53.

ONLINE RESOURCES ON LEARNING DISABILITIES AND FOREIGN LANGUAGES

Schwartz, R. L. (1997). <u>Learning disabilities and foreign language learning: A painful collision</u>. Online: http://www.ldonline.org/ld_indepth/foreign_lang/painful_collision.html.

Sedita, J. (1996). <u>A call for more study skills: Instruction</u>. Online: http://www.ldonline.org/

CHAPTER 3:

DOCUMENTING YOUR LEARNING DISABILITY

Obtaining documentation of your learning disability can be a frustrating issue. This proof of your disability is very important to your college career. You will need official documentation of your learning disability to obtain accommodations when you take standardized tests such as the PSAT, SAT, or ACT. Furthermore, the college you are entering will request proof of your learning disability diagnosis for you to use its services for disabled students or its learning disability or learning center program.

IF YOU HAVE ALREADY BEEN TESTED

Many learning disabled people are diagnosed in high school, usually through the request of a school official such as a teacher, a learning disability specialist, a special education teacher, or a parent. Of course, parental permission is always required for a student to be tested. A trained psychologist or a reading or learning specialist usually administers the test.

Even if you have been tested, it is always wise to call the colleges or universities to which you are applying to find out exactly what they require in terms of documentation. The documentation that you provide to colleges can be **no more than three years old.**

✎ If you were tested in a public school system, the tests that you were given were probably the bare minimum required to qualify you for services in your school district. Therefore, you may find that your college's Office for Disabled Student Services requires additional tests for you to qualify for the services they offer.

✎ If you were tested by a private psychologist, your parents probably paid for it, and it's likely that you got a battery of the latest LD diagnostic tests. These tests should be sufficient evidence of your disability for just about any college. You must check with the office for disabled student services or the learning center at your college to make sure that you have the documentation they request, however.

✎ Public school systems sometimes sends students to a specialist from outside the system to be tested. If your high school referred you to an outside specialist, the school paid for this testing. Schools often use independent contractors if they don't have a psychologist on staff.

IF YOU HAVE NEVER BEEN TESTED

A few different avenues are available for testing if you are ready to enter college but don't have documentation of your learning disability. First, find out from the colleges or universities to which you are applying exactly what you will need. Local agencies in your area may be able either to perform the tests or refer you to diagnosticians. To find the appropriate agencies, check your local telephone book for adult education, adult literacy programs, or literacy councils.

Here are some other places that may help you with testing and diagnosis:

✎ The International Dyslexia Society (formerly the Orton Dyslexia Society)
> 8600 LaSalle Road
> Chester Building, Suite 382
> Baltimore, MD 21286-2044
> 410/296-0232
> 800/222-3123

(There are local chapters nationwide. You can get listings from the international office)

✎ Your state or local vocational rehabilitation agency

✎ Special education programs or study skills classes and reading centers at local colleges

✎ The Disabled Students Services office at your local college or university

✎ Learning Disabilities Association of America

> 4156 Library Road
> Pittsburgh, PA 15234
> 412/341-1515
> Fax: 412/344-0224

✎ Local adult education centers or career centers

✎ Local psychologists listed in the yellow pages

Be sure to ask any relevant questions before you are tested. Remember to include the following crucial points:

✎ What is the cost of the testing?

My Experience: I found out that to receive services, I needed additional testing—to the tune of $1,500!

✎ Will my insurance cover the cost of these tests?

✎ Can I work out a payment plan if I am uninsured or if my insurance will not cover these tests?

✎ Will I get a written report of the diagnosis, results, evaluation, and recommendations?

TYPES OF TESTS

No matter what the orientation of your disability is, experts generally agree that the identification of the learning disability requires a variety of tests and supplementary observations and procedures. If you were given a thorough battery of tests as a child, those results are still significant, especially if they diagnosed your specific learning disability. You will probably need additional testing, however. To familiarize yourself with some of these methods so you won't be totally in the dark when calling a college's disabled students services office or a learning center, I have summarized some of the most widely used tests or screening techniques below. They are divided into several categories (Aptitude/Cognitive, Language, Academic/Achievement test and Specific Assessments of Learning Disabilities/Information Processing.

You never outgrow the learning disability. Under the ADA, the learning disability is life-long. But even though the learning disability will continue, the severity of the condition may change over a period of time. Therefore, if you were tested as child and the results revealed your deficiencies and diagnosis, you will still need to have updated testing and assessments done, particularly assessments used for adults. It is important that these assessments be no more than three years old.

COMMON ASSESSMENTS AND TESTS ADMINISTERED

Aptitude/Cognitive Ability

The Wechsler Adult Intelligence Scale-Revised (WAIS-R). This is a very common one. You may have been administered the children's version as a child. Although this is called an intelligence test, do not let this intimidate you. These tests are used in almost any screening process, and the intelligence quotient (IQ) helps to differentiate between mental retardation and learning disabilities. The scales also provide qualitative information about specific deficiencies in perception and recall of visual patterns, motor difficulties in copying forms, limitations in short-term memory, inability to handle abstract concepts, and many types of language deficiencies. If you are being screened for a learning disability, this may not be the only ones that you will be administered to you.

If you were tested as a child, then you were probably given the WISC-III. You may have even taken the preschool version of this test before you were six years old. But if you were tested in high school (after the age of 16), then you were given the WAIS-R. If you were given the WISC-III, then your college will probably ask you to get tested again. This is probably a good idea, because the WAIS-R will give you a better understanding of your areas of weakness. Knowing your "problem areas" (what you struggle with most) is very helpful when you are preparing to enter college and when you are deciding on your first semester classes.

Parts of the test will probably be difficult for you. The scales were developed without the learning disabled in mind, and are designed more for those who learn through traditional methods. In reality, if the goal is to get an accurate measure of intelligence, this test is not fair to people with learning disabilities. Someone with a learning disability may need paper and pencil to figure out the arithmetic word problems—which are presented orally—but this test does not allow for the test-taker to use pencil and paper. No visual cues will be provided. This test is only one of many that should be used for diagnosing learning disabilities, however.

Stanford-Binet Intelligence Scale (4th ed.). This is another "intelligence" scale that is used as an alternative to the Wechsler, so it is not likely that a battery screening will have both the Stanford-Binet and the Wechsler. The Wechsler is used more widely.

The Kaufman Adolescent and Adult Intelligence Test. This is a multi-subtest battery that covers the age range from 11 years to 85 years. It is based on a model of fluid and crystallized intelligence scales. The crystallized scales measure your ability to solve problems using knowledge. The scales are as follows: Auditory Comprehension, Double Meanings, and Definitions. The fluid scales scale your ability to solve novel problems. The scales are as follows: Rebus Learning, Mystery Codes, and Logical Steps. There is also an expanded battery that includes the following; Memory Block design, Famous Faces, rebus Delayed Recall, and Auditory Delayed Recall.

The Woodcock-Johnson Psychoeducational Battery – Revised: Tests of Cognitive Ability. Both of these test and batteries are used when providing a thorough battery of assessments in order to diagnose a learning disability. These are often found to be used by school psychologists when updating testing for the purpose of the IEP. You may find that you have taken these before. Both of these are widely accepted for the purpose of documentation of a learning disability.

Language Tests

Test Of Adolescent and Adult Language – Third Edition. This is an assessment of receptive and expressive language skills. It will measure listening, speaking, reading, and writing skills.

Test of Written Language – 3 (TOWL-3). This is an assessment of written language skills. It contains essay analysis and traditional formats to assess aspects of written language. It has easy items and is designed to be user friendly for persons with writing disabilities.

Academic/Achievement Test

Scholastic Abilities Test For Adults (SATA).

Stanford Test of Academic Skills (TASK).

Woodcock-Johnson Psychoeducational Battery – Revised: Test of Achievement.

Wechsler Individual Achievement Test (WIAT). All of these test listed above provides assessment of academic achievement. They all look at specific areas of learning. Also assessed is visual and auditory learning. In most cases only one of these will be used.

Specific Assessments for Learning Disabilities/Information Processing

Nelson-Denny reading Skills Test.

Stanford Diagnostic Mathematics Test.

Woodcock Reading Mastery Test – Revised.

Detroit Test of Learning Aptitude – Adult (DTLA-A). The tests listed above are looking at specific mental abilities. They are designed to identify students who need special help and to document specific areas of strength or weakness and to monitor how effective accommodation and remedial efforts will be to improve performance. More than one of these may be utilized during your assessment.

It is important to note that not all of the above mentioned assessments will be utilized. Primarily this provides you with an overview the basics as far as what kind of evaluations are out there. Do not be afraid of them and ask questions as often as you need to.

Testing professionals may use any number of less formal screening techniques. One of these is an Informal Reading Inventory. In this test, a student will be asked to read passages silently or aloud, and listen to as passages are read to him or her. If the student is reading out loud, the examiner will listen for any miscues, or mistakes. The reading of each passage is following by a comprehension check, which may include questions about vocabulary, facts, main ideas, inferences, and sequences.

Keep in mind that it is your right to know the results of any test that is administered to you. Tell the test administrator that you expect a consultation afterwards. Some school districts and testing facilities require that your parent or legal guardian be present at such a consultation if you are under 18 years of age, but remember that you have a right to be there as well.

Also, be sure that the person interpreting your tests is familiar with learning disabilities in your age range—child, adolescent, or adult. The people who can interpret your results are psychologists, rehabilitation counselors, learning and reading specialists, and LD specialists. Where and in what situation you are tested will determine whether or not you will have one, some, or all of the professionals listed above involved in the evaluation and interpretation of your tests. The term learning disability is defined as a significant gap between a person's intelligence and the skills the person has achieved at each age. For documentation purposes, you must be able to meet this definition.

SOME TERMS USED IN TEST RESULTS

The following are some terms you may hear in the discussion of your test results. These definitions may help you in understanding your diagnosis a little better.

Diagnostic tests: This series of formal and informal measures of skills and abilities, including general levels of intelligence and academic skill, is designed to identify your strengths and weaknesses and to assist in finding ways to help you learn and work more effectively.

Norm: This term is used a lot by test administrators when they are reading your scores back. They may say, "Well, your score falls between these norms." One important step in standardizing a test is establishing norms. Many of the tests used to diagnose learning disabilities have no predetermined standards of passing or failing. In most cases, a person's test score is interpreted by comparing it with the scores of other people of the same age on the same test. Therefore, the norm is the normal or average performance. For example, if the average 17-year-old gets 77 out of 100 problems correct on a test, then the norm score for a 17-year-old is 77.

Normal: Although I hate this word, you will often hear it when talking to college administrators. They may say, "Well, we really need to see how you will perform compared to **normal** college freshmen with your major." Or from professors: "If I give you extra time on the exam, that will interfere with the academic integrity of the course that the **normal** students are challenged with." When this word is used, it implies that those who are learning disabled are **not** normal. If you hear this term, correct the speaker and assert that you are just as normal as those average students. You just learn differently and need a different method of teaching and test taking.

Criterion-referenced: This term simply means that the validity of the instrument (the test) is measured against a criterion or standard. Therefore, test performance may be measured in terms of the specific kinds of mathematical skills mastered, the difficulty level of the reading material comprehended, or the estimated vocabulary size. In this way, a specified content area is used as an interpretive frame of reference for the instrument, instead of a specified population of test-takers.

Standardization: This term implies the uniformity of procedure in administering and scoring the test. Telling people that you "don't do well on standardized tests" is a very logical thing to say, because a standardized test is given just that way—the standard way. Therefore, because you don't learn in the traditional or standard way, you probably don't perform well on a standardized test. You will, however, do better with a **dynamic assessment** or some sort of accommodation, like taking a test orally or using a scribe.

Dynamic assessment: This term may be used to explain your scores. Basically, it means that there was an intentional departure from the traditional or standardized way in which your test was administered.

My Experience: I hate taking tests; I don't test well. But there were times when I had to be tested, just as you have been or will be. The last time I was tested, my examiner used this dynamic assessment method, so I had a better opportunity to show what I could do. Then I was tested without the dynamic assessment, so the administrator could compare the scores. Using testing methods that deviated slightly from the traditional ones made a big difference for me. For example, since I am a very tactile and visual learner, allowing me to use paper and pencil for the math section helped me do much better. Having this option to work out the math problems physically gave me the same level playing field as test takers who don't have a learning disability.

Attention Deficit Hyperactive Disorder (ADHD) or Hyperactivity: A person with ADHD moves constantly and is restless much of the time. This person talks a lot and many times has incomplete thoughts, because his or her thoughts often run together. Sometimes this person may have poor motor control and coordination. This person also gets frustrated quickly, can be moody, and is easily distracted.

Hypoactivity: The hypoactive individual works and reacts slowly. This person appears unemotional and will hang onto a task even when it is completed.

Attention Deficit Disorder (ADD): Someone with ADD has many of the same symptoms as someone with ADHD, but without the hyperactivity. For example, a person with ADD daydreams and is confused much of the time and never seem to finish tasks or projects. He or she gets bored very easily; concentration for this person is a monumental task. Distracted by other people and by outside noises, this person can be moody and unpredictable.

FOR FURTHER READING

Lyon, R. (1994). <u>Frames of reference for the assessment of learning disabilities: New views on measurement issues</u>. Baltimore, MD: Paul H. Brookes Publishing.

Kavale, K. & Forness, S. (1995). <u>The nature of learning disabilities: Critical elements of diagnosis and classification</u>. Hillsdale, NJ: Lawrence Erbaum.

CHAPTER 4:
TAKING THE SAT OR ACT

THE SAT

As a sophomore in high school, I remember seeing a friend of mine very intently reading a study guide for the Preliminary Scholastic Aptitude Test (PSAT). This test helps you practice for taking the SAT and is the National Merit Scholarship qualifying test. I was not registered to take the PSAT.

My friend told me that I should have registered to take the PSAT, so I would have an idea of what to expect on the SAT. I wanted to say, "get a life," but I knew deep in my heart that she **would** have a life, probably of a much better quality than mine, because at that time I didn't even know if I was going to graduate from high school.

Administered since 1926 by the Educational Testing Service (ETS), the Scholastic Aptitude Test is the college entrance exam most often required for college admission. When I was in high school, I remember dreading the SAT. I was intimidated by tests anyway, as are most learning-disabled individuals, but this was an important timed exam—even scarier!

Any person with a documented learning disability can get accommodations for taking the PSAT and the SAT, including extra time. If I could do it again, I would take the PSAT. Had I gone into the SAT knowing what to expect, I might have done better on it. Also, had I known that I was entitled to take extra time, or request a reader on the test, I would have done so.

Tips and Useful Information

✎ You and your counselor should start the application process early for taking the PSAT and/or the SAT using accommodations. I recommend beginning this process the spring before the year you are planning to take the test.

✎ You must get a "common eligibility form" from the College Board. The College Board Services for Students with Disabilities (SSD) provides testing accommodations for the SAT as well as the PSAT.

✎ You can use this form for all tests administered by the College Board. The school also completes a part of this form.

✎ Once approved, you will be sent a letter of eligibility that states that you can have accommodations. Your school will get a copy of this letter as well.

✎ Examples of the types of accommodations you might be given are extended time, a proctor or reader, and specific color background and/or foreground for certain visual and reading disabilities.

✎ You can also have computer and technology accommodations if you are taking the computer-based test. These kinds of accommodations, however, have to be specified and documented.

✎ You can use alternate testing formats.

✎ In all cases, you must be able to meet all the requirements for documentation of your learning disability.

✎ Your testing must be current (not older than three years), done by a qualified professional, and a specific diagnosis must be included.

✎ You should know that the testing professional must also make recommendations for accommodations and give the reasons for making them. Most importantly, the documentation must indicate that your learning disability substantially limits the major life function of learning.

✎ You should pay close attention to registration deadlines for test applications. Often those who are requesting accommodations must register early.

✎ You should be sure to consult the ETS web site, http://www.ets.org, before you begin this process to see if the Office of Disability has made any changes in its policies.

✎ You can also study my chapter on documentation.

THE ACT

The American College Test (ACT) is your other choice for an admissions test. First given in 1959, the ACT is administered by the American College Testing Program, based in Iowa City. The ACT is most often used by colleges in the Midwest and western United States, and less often used by colleges on the east coast. Some colleges allow you to take either the SAT or the ACT.

My Experience: If you have a choice, I recommend taking the ACT. It seemed to be more "user-friendly" than the SAT. I scored higher on it, as did most of the other students with learning disabilities I have talked to.

Tips and Useful Information

✎ You and your counselor should start the application process early for taking the ACT and/or the P-ACT utilizing accommodations. I recommend beginning this process the spring before the year you are planning on taking the test.

✎ You must provide documentation just as you would for accommodations in college. The ACT Office of Services for Students with

Disabilities states on its web site that "if you currently receive accommodations in school due to a professionally diagnosed and documented disability, you may provide documentation to support your request for accommodations."

✎ You should familiarize yourself with the following available accommodations.

Types of accommodations:

Standard Time-National Testing with Accommodations. ACT refers to this as Option #1. This means that you CAN take the test with the standard time limits BUT you use either a standard or large print test booklet, and your disability requires accommodations at the testing location, for example, a room with no distractions by others taking the test. Using this option means your test scores will be marked "National." I explain this kind of marking later as "Flagging the Test."

Documentation for this option specifically requires that you have a professional explain the nature of your disability in detail and the accommodations that you normally receive in school.

Extended-Time National Testing. ACT refers to this as Option #2. This means that you can test at a regularly scheduled test center and use either a standard or large print test booklet, but you require additional time due to your professionally diagnosed and documented disability. Using this option means that your test scores will be marked "Special." The extended time allotted is up to five hours total testing time, including your breaks between test sections. This is more than time and a half—the standard for extended time on a standardized test. This option usually means that you will be assigned a separate room and a private proctor.

Documentation consists of a special application you and your school official fill out. This application will require your diagnosis and the appropriate documentation.

Non-National Testing Option. This option is good if you normally—meaning in your current school situation—use more that 50% additional time for tests, or you require testing over more than one day because of your disability, or you alternate test formats such as using a reader or an audio cassette. This option means that your test scores will be marked "Special."

Documentation requires that you and your school official have to complete a request for ACT Assessment Special Testing. This request should include documentation of your diagnosed disability and all supporting information. Your school officials and/or counselors can obtain all special forms and applications. I recommend that you look at the ACT web site, http://www.act.org, for updated information on policies regarding testing accommodations and registration.

I cannot overemphasize the importance of knowing your legal entitlements. The ADA is behind you, and you should let the two administering organizations know that even though they cannot "norm" the scores of learning disabled students, you are still entitled to take these tests with accommodations.

If you or your school counselor and school officials have any questions about the procedures for registering for these tests or obtaining accommodations, contact the two administering organizations:

> American College Testing Program
> P. O. Box 168
> Iowa City, IA 5224
> 319/337-1000
> www.act.org
>
> Educational Testing Service
> P. O. Box 6000
> Princeton, NJ 08541-6000
> 609/921-9000
> www.ets.org

FLAGGING AND DISCLOSURE

It is important to realize that when you take either the SAT or the ACT with accommodations for your learning disability, your test scores will be "flagged" or specially marked. This means that your results will include a statement about the testing conditions. For example, as I stated in the section regarding the ACT, if you take the test using option one, your scores will be marked "national." To the college or university, this means that you took this test using the standard time given in national testing with accommodations.

The marking of your scores as "Special" tells the college or university that you took the test using the extended time option or the special testing with extended time and alternate test formats.

In the SAT, scores are marked or flagged as "Nonstandard Administration." If the test is administered with accommodations that do not require nonstandard time conditions, such as large print test or just a private room, then the scores are marked as "Non-Standard."

Other than these markings on reported scores, your disability and any other information that you provide is strictly confidential. The college or university should not and cannot ask you about your disability at the interview. You may want to disclose this information at the interview anyway to show how you have compensated for your disability and survived 12 years of education.

You may want to disclose the disability on your application in the essay section. This way you have another opportunity to focus on your abilities despite your disabilities. If the college you want to enter requires that you apply to a separate LD program to get the services you need, then you will be disclosing to them of course. Separate programs for LD students are discussed in Chapter 5.

I know it seems unfair that your scores are marked differently because you are learning disabled, but keep in mind that because you will take your test under different conditions, your scores will be different. When these standardized tests are "normed" or studied in statistical reports on average SAT scores at a certain college or university, your scores cannot be considered in those statistics simply because you took them in a nonstandard way. You are NOT part of the so-called NORM here.

CHAPTER 5:

FINDING THE RIGHT COLLEGE FOR YOU

To find out whether something is right for you, you have to ask the right questions. When you buy a stereo, you probably ask lots of questions to find one that suits your needs, and the same is true when you are buying a car or any other "big ticket" item. Think of college as a big ticket item. When you are looking for a college, you are in the market for an education, and you should go to a school suited to your needs. You may be able to get into an Ivy League school, but if that school does not have the services to help you do well there, then it is not the right place for you. You must get accurate and complete information before you commit to any college or university.

Your choice of a college should be one that you feel strongly about. College is not just a place to get an education, but a home and lifestyle for four years or more. I went to many schools before I finally ended up at the university from which I graduated. That school not only had the services I needed, but a supportive environment in which I knew I could live and learn until I accomplished my goal.

As you make your choice, don't convince yourself that just because one college accepts you, that it is the only college that will. Take your time in making this decision. It is one that will affect you for at least the next four years—and possibly for the rest of your life. Here are some things you should consider before you make your final decision:

DOES THIS COLLEGE HAVE A LEARNING DISABILITIES PROGRAM OR DOES IT PROVIDE SERVICES FOR THE LEARNING DISABLED UNDER GENERAL DISABLED SERVICES?

This question is often a confusing one, because colleges can define learning disabilities programs in several different ways. Some colleges provide services for the learning disabled but no separate program for people with learning disabilities. Here is how I see the difference:

Learning disability program or structured program: A specific, full-time college or university program catering to the needs of the clinically recognized LD student. A college or university with a full-time program will usually have a full-time learning disability specialist, as well as the latest learning disability technology. A college with a specific LD program may have less technology and fewer services for people with learning disabilities than a school with a general student services office, however. Never assume that services will be provided.

Learning disability services: These services may appear at the college or university under one of the following headings: Disabled Student Services, Reading and Study Skills Laboratory, Educational Development, or Tutorial Services. The difference between such a service and the type previously described is that this service is not specifically for the learning disabled. This department or division of student services provides accommodations and assistance to all recognized disabilities, and therefore, this service may not provide the latest equipment or a learning disabilities specialist. But the school is still required to provide "reasonable accommodations" for any disabled student, including those with learning disabilities.

WHICH IS BETTER: A COLLEGE WITH A PROGRAM SPECIFICALLY GEARED TOWARD LEARNING DISABLED STUDENTS, OR A SCHOOL THAT JUST HAS LEARNING DISABILITY SERVICES?

Whether one school is better than another really depends on the college. Some colleges have great LD programs, but others have even better Disabled Student Services (DSS) departments. You must find out what makes a particular program special and whether it meets **your** needs.

You do need to be able to recognize what you need in terms of support at a college or university. You will be able to do this by knowing your disability and how you learn best. If you are attending IEP meetings, this should be discussed. Listen to what is being said and what strategies are being put in place—this will help you decide what your needs are. Some if not all of these strategies can be duplicated at the college or university. For example, if you are utilizing a note taker in your classes, chances are you will need one in your college classes as well. I cannot stress enough the need to know how you learn and how you learn best.

My Experience: The college where I finally received my bachelor's and my master's degrees did not have a separate learning disabilities program. It did have very good services for disabled students, however, and by my senior year, it served more students with learning disabilities than students with any other disabilities. It also made a reading and writing center available for all students and had up-to-date adaptive equipment and computers. Most importantly, it had a learning disabilities specialist on staff. This department was the reason why I made it through college.

IF THE COLLEGE OR UNIVERSITY HAS A SEPARATE LD PROGRAM, DO I NEED TO APPLY TO THAT PROGRAM AS WELL AS TO THE COLLEGE?

Often, such a program requires an admission procedure separate from that of the university or college. In most cases, you have to be admitted to the school before you are accepted in the LD program. Other students have been accepted to the LD program but rejected from the university itself. The answer to this question is important because you need to know if you will have to fill out two separate applications, and if so, whether you have different requirements and/or deadlines for each. You must call and speak to a staff person in the LD program.

WHAT DOES THE COLLEGE OR UNIVERSITY REQUIRE IN TERMS OF DOCUMENTATION TO RECEIVE SERVICES?

You can get the answer to this question by calling the DSS office or LD program and speaking to the LD specialist or the person in charge of checking LD documentation. What assessments or tests does the school require as proof of a learning disability? A basic rule here is the test should **not** be over three years old.

DOES THE COLLEGE HAVE AN ADDED FEE FOR USE OF THE SERVICES FOR THE LEARNING DISABLED?

Believe it or not, some colleges require an additional payment for these services. Often this charge is to pay for tutors, a fee that non-learning disabled students also have to pay. On the other hand, these services are **your** accommodations. Do the colleges require the wheelchair-bound students to pay an additional fee for the use of wheelchair ramps? Since the passage of the ADA, students may begin to contest such fees in court to force colleges to waive or totally remove this fee. Having a disability should not mean you acquire an extra tax or fee.

If the college justifies this extra fee as payment for tutors and study skills classes for LD students, then I advise you to use the tutorial services to the limit, and request a tutor who has experience working with LD students. And go to those study skills classes!

DOES THE COLLEGE OR UNIVERSITY PROVIDE ANY OF THE FOLLOWING ACCOMMODATIONS: TEST PROCTORS; EXTENDED TIME ON EXAMS; OPTIONS TO TAKE ORAL, RATHER THAN WRITTEN EXAMS; NOTETAKERS; USE OF TAPE RECORDERS IN CLASS; TEXTBOOKS ON TAPE OR READERS FOR TEXTS; USE OF COMPUTER SCREEN READING SYSTEMS; OR ADVANCED SPEECH SYNTHESIZERS?

These services and accommodations can make or break your success in college. Ask if the school provides these and any other services that will help you. If you need a multisensory approach to learning, find out what kind the college offers. For example, does the college provide hands-on learning opportunities in the curriculum—opportunities that allow for tactile as well as didactic learning? Can you utilize a note taker and tape record the class as well? Speak to the LD specialist if there is one on staff, or speak to the director of the program

WHAT EQUIPMENT, IF ANY, DOES THE COLLEGE OR UNIVERSITY HAVE FOR LD STUDENTS? ASK FOR SPECIFICS. DOES THE COLLEGE OR UNIVERSITY HAVE A KURZWEIL READER ON CAMPUS? A TALKING COMPUTER? A VOICE RECOGNITION SYSTEM? A REAL-TIME SPELL CHECKER?

Equipment and computer software can make a difference in the way you learn and the speed with which you do so. See Chapter 6 for a discussion of this and for a more complete list of equipment that will be helpful.

DOES THIS COLLEGE OFFER CURRICULUM MODIFICATION?

The answer to this question can make a big difference for you. In other words, can you take another class instead of a foreign language? Or can a person with dyscalcula substitute a statistics requirement with a less complicated math course? LD students often drop out of school because they can't pass foreign language or math courses. Ask about what modifications will be available to you as a student with a learning disability It is very important.

My Experience: I was given the option of taking a class in foreign culture instead of a foreign language. Since I had already failed several foreign language classes, I cannot tell you how happy that made me. This opportunity was one of the things that helped save my college career.

DOES THE COLLEGE HAVE AN OPTION FOR COMPLETING A FOUR-YEAR DEGREE PROGRAM IN FIVE YEARS OR LONGER?

Many LD students (as well as others) find it difficult to take a full course load, and this can make it hard to complete a degree in four years. As a result, some colleges now offer a five-year program option. Knowing that you have the option of additional time can relieve some of the stress of your college experience.

 **My Experience:** It took me seven years to finish my bachelor's degree. Please remember, however, that this was my experience; this is not the average time for a student with a learning disability.

Keep in mind there can be financial ramifications regarding financial aid and taking longer than four years to graduate. Talk to your financial aid office. this is very important!

DOES THE COLLEGE HAVE AN LD SUPPORT GROUP OR LD RESOURCE GROUP?

You may benefit from getting together with other LD students once a week or twice or month. This is a group in which you can discuss such things as getting through a particular class or dealing with a particular professor.

Such a group can help you find out which professors understand different learning styles and which ones are less accommodating as you select your courses. It also helps just to learn that you are not the only student having these difficulties and that others know what it's like to struggle through a class and still get just a "C."

This group can also act as a social vehicle for you: you will have a chance to make friends and to feel comfortable being around other people with the same or similar difficulties.

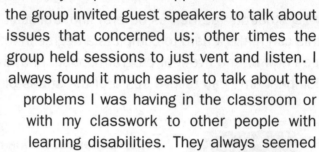

My Experience: I found the group at my college to be extremely helpful and supportive. Sometimes the group invited guest speakers to talk about issues that concerned us; other times the group held sessions to just vent and listen. I always found it much easier to talk about the problems I was having in the classroom or with my classwork to other people with learning disabilities. They always seemed to know what I was talking about. The group also created an "underground" list of professors to stay away from.

I have created a checklist with these questions that you can photocopy to use when calling or visiting colleges and universities. You can find this checklist in Appendix A on page 101.

OTHER OPTIONS: COMMUNITY OR JUNIOR COLLEGES

One option that you should not rule out is the community college, called a junior college in some areas. This college generally offers two-year programs with degrees that range from an associate's (AA) degree to a technical certificate.

The programs are generally quite varied, and the community college can offer a very supportive environment to the LD student. Furthermore, the community college can build a foundation from which to transfer to a four-year college and obtain a bachelor's degree. The classes in community colleges are usually smaller and give students more opportunities to meet one-on-one with professors.

My Experience: The community college I attended did not have a learning disability specialist or a learning disability center, but one counselor was responsible for all the disabled students. At this college, I arranged for all my exams ahead of time and took them in the counseling center with a proctor, who was usually the counselor. I enjoyed the smaller classes and I got more individual attention from the instructors.

Often, a student—whether or not he or she has a learning disability—will choose to go to a community college before attending a four-year program because the costs are lower. You should keep college expenses in mind because, as a learning disabled student, you may take longer than four years to finish a bachelor's degree. If so, you will have more than four years of tuition bills or student loans to pay back. To keep those costs down, you might consider a two-year program, if just for financial reasons. The quality of the education at an accredited two-year college can be just as high and can help prepare you for a four-year college or university. Moreover, most four-year institutions will accept up to 60 credits for transfer from a two-year college. Four-year colleges usually require around 120 credits to graduate, so transferring 60 credits into a school will put you well on your way to a degree. You might want to check with your intended four-year college, however. The specifics of what will transfer and what will not vary from school to school. You don't want to have to repeat classes, which can be time-consuming and expensive.

In many cases, when you attend a community or junior college and you earn 30 credits or more and then transfer to a four-year college, you will not need SAT scores. A four-year college or university will admit on the basis of your grades in the courses you transfer.

While many two-year colleges may not have a learning disabilities specialist, a learning disability center, or services specifically geared toward LD students on campus, you still have the right to accommodations for your learning disability at community colleges, just as you do at a four-year college or university. Any community college probably has an office for disabled students, so be sure to tell your advisor or counselor about your diagnosis, and be sure to provide documentation of it.

The community college is also an option if you want to take a class in the summer. When you return home from your college or university, or even before you return, look into the summer schedule at the local community college. The summer is a perfect time for taking a class you need at time when you don't have to worry about all your other classes.

Furthermore, a community college near your college or university may offer a class you are required to take during a time when your college doesn't offer it. To make sure that the class is equivalent to the one at your institution, you will need to get approval from your college advisor and/or the department head for your major to take the class. This is usually just a matter of bringing in the class description from the community college catalogue. It's a good idea to get this approval before you register for the class, though, to make sure it's equivalent to the required class at your college or university.

Most importantly, the community college is a place to get remedial work, which is a good thing to know.

FEEL PASSIONATE ABOUT YOUR SCHOOL CHOICE

This is very important! I strongly advocate that you visit the schools you are applying to before you make a final choice. Decide what learning climate will be best for you, not just what your parents or your friends recommend to you. **You** are the one who will have to be there for four or more years and **you** will be the one expected to succeed.

RESOURCES TO HELP YOU

Many colleges can cater to your specific learning needs. The following are two guides that list and evaluate colleges with services for the learning disabled.

The K & W Guide to Colleges for the Learning Disabled (4th ed.), by Marybeth
   Kraviets and Imy F. Wax. (1998). New York: Harper Perennial.

   This guide is the best you can buy. It is very complete and easy to follow. What
   many authors and editors of guides like these do not realize is that often the LD

student is the reader, so the guide must be easy to read and to follow. The authors of this guide have written it with the learning disabled reader in mind.

The K & W Guide gives a full description of the colleges in an easy-to-follow format. For every school listed, it covers 66 points on everything from the type of support the college provides (learning disability structured program or coordinated services), to the kind of athletic program it has. It also gives such vital information as the kind of LD equipment (such as Kurzweil Readers) provided and the availability of textbooks on tape or of readers to tape textbooks. The guide also gives tuition and housing information. In addition, it lists two-year colleges. Over all, it is very thorough and complete.

Peterson's Colleges with Programs for Students with Learning Disabilities, by Charles T. Mangrum II & Stephen S. Strichart (1997). Princeton, NJ: Peterson's Guides, Inc.

This guide is much harder to follow and is really geared for the school counselor, not the student. The guide's best point, however, is that it is divided into two sections: one listing colleges with comprehensive programs and the other listing colleges with special services. It is fairly thorough and gives such information as whether colleges offer alternative exam arrangements and whether it has a learning disabled support group. It is also helpful to those serving the LD population. A bonus CD is included.

PART TWO

SURVIVING COLLEGE

Classroom 102

CHAPTER 6:
ASSISTIVE TECHNOLOGY FOR THE LEARNING DISABLED

More new technologies to assist the learning disabled are being designed every day. Just since I finished graduate school in 1995, a flood of new products has entered the marketplace. Some of these technologies were originally developed for the deaf, the hearing impaired, or the visually impaired, but these technologies can often benefit the learning disabled population as well.

Keeping up on the latest equipment and knowing what technology will suit your learning needs can be a full-time job. One helpful resource for this information is Technology for Students with Learning Disabilities, edited by K. Higgins and R. Boone. Its collection of articles focusing on the use of computer technology for the learning disabled can be a valuable resource in purchasing adaptive technology for college. The articles are useful not only in an educational setting, but in the workplace as well, as it is written for a diverse audience, including educators, researchers, and manufacturers, as well as parents and adults with learning disabilities.

MULTISENSORY APPROACHES TO READING

Books on Tape

One option that helped save me in college was books on tape from Recordings for the Blind and Dyslexic (RFB&D). Originally called Recordings for the Blind, the organization changed its name as more people with learning disabilities began to use this service. When I first heard about this service, I thought, "I'm not blind. What could this organization do for me?" It didn't take long to figure it out. Some learning disabled people don't perceive written words in a way they can easily read. The words on the page appear jumbled or backward and fall off the page. We can't keep our place and often end up reading the same line for an hour. The beauty of books on tape is that you can listen instead. I find it helpful to listen and follow along with my finger or with a blocker of some sort.

The way RFB&D works is pretty simple. You'll need to send an application that will register you as an RFB&D user (see the end of this chapter for contact information). You must pay a one-time fee to register and an annual membership fee. In addition, the organization requires a disability statement certifying that you do indeed qualify for their services. This statement can come from your Disabled Student Services coordinator, the learning disability specialist who works with you at your college or school, your vocational rehabilitation counselor, or your high school special education teacher or counselor. After you are registered with RFB&D, you can submit requests for books on tape for the rest of your school career. The tapes are shipped at no cost to you, and other than the cost of membership, the service is free. You are **borrowing** these tapes; return labels will be enclosed so you can ship them back to RFB&D when you are done with them. There is no set time limit; RFB&D expects that you will be borrowing a textbook throughout a semester. You will receive reminders, however, that you have a **borrowed** book.

Occasionally, RFB&D will not have a textbook that you need; if so, the organization will write you to let you know. Often, they will have a different edition than the one you required for your course. If this is the case, check with the Office of Disabled Student Services (DSS) at your school to see if they can provide readers for you. Sometimes DSS has work-study students who proctor test sessions and record textbooks on tapes for the visually impaired and for learning-disabled students.

It is extremely important to request books from RFB&D well in advance, because it takes a long time to get the tapes shipped to you. This delay is especially long if the textbook is not already taped or if they need your approval to record a different edition of the book.

In 1991, RFB&D merged with **Computerized Books for the Blind (CBFB)** and expanded their library by more than 200 titles available on computer diskettes. The computerized text costs on average $15 to $20 per title, but it is yours to keep and does not have to be mailed back.

Tape Players and Other Accessories

Tapes (as opposed to computer disks) from RFB&D require a special kind of tape player that plays 15/16 inches per second (IPS) to accommodate two or four tracks. Your public library or school library probably has one that you can borrow.

Those who are eligible for services of the National Library Service for the Blind and Physically Handicapped (NLS), a division of the U.S. Library of Congress, can request the playback equipment on loan for as long as patrons use the NLS library service. You go to your local library or school library and ask if you can apply for NLS borrowing services. The NLS will allow only RFB&D borrowers and patrons of NLS to borrow equipment. You should consult your regional NLS network library for more information (see the end of this chapter for the address.) NLS also has a buying guide that lists all the known sources for adaptive equipment, available through the same address.

The American Printing House for the Blind (APH) also sells tape players and accessories. These tape players are a good option, because they also record and can be used to tape class lectures as well. The players sold through APH are easy to carry around. The equipment from NLS tends to be much older; bulkier versions of the 4-track cassette players that are impossible to carry around in your bookbag. For information on the price, size, and availability of equipment, you can contact the APH at the address and phone number at the end of this chapter.

Another source for this type of equipment is Boston Information and Technology Corporation (BIT). BIT also sells models that are convenient to carry. The two models are called the Talkman II and the Talkman III. The address and phone number are listed at the end of this chapter.

RFB&D also sells the tape players you need for these tapes. They have four portable models to choose from that are portable and also carry four desktop models. You will need to contact them for pricing.

The Kurzweil Reader

The **Kurzweil Reader,** by Xerox® , is a computer that scans printed material and then reads aloud, in one of six voices chosen by the user, what it has scanned. Although it was developed mainly for use by the visually impaired, the reader is extremely useful to LD students.

My Experience: My university purchased the Kurzweil Reader for the visually impaired. However, the LD students certainly made good use of it. Many times, I would realize that I didn't have a reader for some articles that I needed to read by my next class, sometimes by that afternoon. So I would go to the library where the equipment was kept and put my article on the scanner, pick the voice, the speed, and the format—and bingo! The article was read to me. I frequently brought a tape recorder so that I could tape the reading as well. It was fast and easy.

The Kurzweil Reader is an invaluable piece of technology. Be sure to find out if your college has this or something similar available for students.

USEFUL COMPUTER SOFTWARE PROGRAMS

The market is literally exploding with LD friendly software. There is so much out there that, by the time you read this, there will be even more than the ones I mention. Also keep in mind that the ones I mention are ones that I like. This does not mean that they will work for you. I know what my needs are in an educational setting and now a work setting, so I look at software that I am (1) familiar with, and (2) will fit my needs. You are the consumer here, so be absolutely certain that the product you buy will be the one that works for you. You should try it out and get all the information you can on the product before you make that purchase.

I am going to talk about only a few software programs. It will give you an idea of what is out there and what types of things to look for. Software programs that assist you in writing and reading are the ones I will focus on.

One of the most popular in this category is DragonDictate™ Naturally Speaking Preferred V4.0. This is a continuous speech voice recognition software that types what you dictate. It supports virtually all Windows " applications. You are able to train the program with your voice in five minutes. When you speak into it, your voice is transcribed almost immediately and appears as text on the screen. Most importantly, you can use this for your reports and papers, but you can even use this for your e-mail. The program can be ordered on line or purchased at an office supply or computer store.

My Experience: When I was in college as a graduate student, I was introduced to a program called Soundproof. Since the university purchased the system, students were allowed to check out the laptop computers with SoundProof and to take them to classes to take notes and exams. We were also allowed to use them for writing papers. This program allowed me to hear what I was typing. As I would type, the speech synthesizer would speak and the highlighter would highlight each word. This allowed me to hear what I was typing. With a set of headphones, I was golden during essay exams or taking notes in class.

My writing certainly improved when I used the system—and I even **enjoyed** writing more. I had become so tired of WordPerfect• telling me that it could not recognize a word in spellcheck. With this system, I can often hear my misspellings. Another advantage is the highlighting, which really helps me to stay focused and not lose my place as often.

The SoundProof program is now out of production, but there are others on the market that do similar things. Humanware, the company that produced SoundProof, is currently producing other packages that re-create the abilities of SoundProof. I suggest calling them at the phone number provided at the end of the chapter and seeing what is available. This company is on the leading edge of disabilities and technology.

Kurzweil 3000 is a new tool that reads scanned or electronic test aloud using a human sounding synthetic speech. The words are highlighted in contrast as they are spoken. This patented auditory and visual presentation of information helps increase reading accuracy, speed and reading comprehension for you if you are struggling through reading. This is put out by Learnout & Hauspie. This piece of software requires the following: processor with 166 MHz or faster, 32 MB, 120 to 150 MB of hard disc space, video ram of 2 MB or more, screen resolution of 800 X 600 pixels, High Color Palette, Windows 95, 98 2000, or Windows NT, a TWAIN compliant scanner, a Creative labs Sound Blaster 16 or 16 bit compliant sound card, a CD Drive, keyboard, mouse and floppy disc drive. The prices I have seen are pretty steep, but from the testimonials I have heard, very much worth it. I have found a few colleges that have this available for the students to use, so you should be sure to ask.

Another voice recognition program I am familiar with is L&H VoiceXpress Advanced Version 4. I have not seen this in stores but on the Internet. Computernerds carries this at www.computernerdz.com. It is reported by computer magazines as being the state-of-voice recognition for writing reports, letters, and pretty much anything else you will need for school. It reports that it will allow for dictation into all Windows applications and offers what is called Natural Language Technology capabilities. It also works with Microsoft Word 2000. You can teach it your voice in virtually minutes. This program will dictate, format, and edit. It has continuous speech technology, with 98% accuracy. The flexibility in the Natural Language Technology (NLT) allows you to use a variety of commands and still get the results you want for your end product. It requires at least Windows 95, a processor equivalent to Intel Pentium with MMX, 200 Mhz, 32 MB RAM, 160 MB free space on your hard drive, Creative Labs Sound Blaster 16, CD-ROM Drive, and speakers. It is fairly inexpensive.

Via Voice Standard is a voice-to-text system that has been on the market for a while. It is very affordable and easy to install. I have actually used this in the work place and very grateful I did. My supervisor was too. It requires a short training time and has very fast text entry. It has a neat feature called

"Analyze Mt Documents" which learns and remembers how you write. It can creat voice short cuts for frequently used words or commands. It has automatic formatting for currency, weights, phone and other numbers. You can correct, edit and format using your voice. It will operate with Microsoft Windows 98, Intel Pentium, 166 MHz with MMX and 265 K L2 cache or equivalent, 48 MB RAM, 260 MB hard disc space, Quad Speed CD-Rom Driver, Display mode set to 256 colors or higher, 16-bit card with microphone input jack and good recording capability, external speakers. The price on the Internet was significantly lower than in the store—a major issue for the starving student!

I had the pleasure of trying out an icon-driven, point-and-click interface called WYNN Interface at an educational conference. This is produced by Arkenstone. It has been field-tested on LD students and adults. It transforms printed text into understandable text. It allows you to modify your entire computer interface to suit your needs, using your "strengths to strengthen your weaknesses." It will spotlight each word as it reads it out loud. Arkenstone calls this "bimodal approach with simultaneous visual and auditory input." You can shut the voice off if you prefer only the visual input. You can also change the size and spacing of text. If you find following word to word difficult, then the WYNN program can mask out distracting sections of the page or change the color of the cursor. You can easily high light and insert book marks. You can add written or spoken notes so that you can summarize important passages or sections. The tool bar is rotating and reads the functions to you. Intuitive buttons and icons give you a short learning curve. The dual auditory and visual presentation is probably one of the best features, and the color-coded tool bar is also very user friendly. All the speech can be modified to fit your needs. It requires a Pentium PC, with at least Windows 95, VGA video card and monitor capable of 640 X 480 resolution, 256 color mode, 32 MB of RAM, 100 MB free space for the program plus additional for document storage, CD-Rom, and microphone. It will recognize MS Word, Word Perfect, HTML, and many more. It comes with Via Voice. Most scanners can be used with WYNN. Arkenstone will let you try this for 30 days with a money-back guarantee and also provides a one-year warranty. It can be ordered from an Arkenstone dealer, whose toll-free number is listed at the end of this chapter. You should ask them about a demonstration

As I stated earlier, HumanWare does have some cutting edge software out. The speech to text technology that is offered is Keynote GOLD Speech Synthesis. This is a very high quality program designed extreme pronunciation accuracy and clarity. This is referred to as multi media speech software. It is reported to specifically be designed to cope with the inconsistencies of the English Language. It will run on Windows 3.1 or 3.11 and Windows 95 or 98. The prices can be found by contacting HumanWare at 1-800-722-3393.

HumanWare has also come up with a "Palmtop Solution," the Keynote Companion Series II. This is a portable information management system designed specifically for people with visual impairment. But because of the speech synthesizing capabilities, the LD population will find it user friendly. It uses Keysoft software and Keynote GOLD speech. It was designed specifically for voice output and is very user-friendly. It is like a palm computer with a voice synthesizer. The Keysoft is the screen reading program. It will check spelling with Keyspell; You can balance your checkbook with Keyplus; You can schedule or review your appointments or classes with Keyplan. It is the Palm Pilot for the LD student! HumanWare can be contacted directly for the current list price.

TextHELP is another product from HumanWare. This is designed specifically for persons with reading and writing difficulties. It features screen reading, advanced phonetic spell checker, contextual word prediction, abbreviation expansion, a log that will record typical spelling errors for future analysis, and homophone support. This is the ability to store in a separate database, 1,4000 homophones that can be spoken out loud. This assists in reducing the confusion with similar sounding words. It requires an IBM compatible PC, Pentium 120 with a soundcard, speakers and 40 MB of disc space. It will work with Windows 3. and Windows 95 but must have 16 MB of free disc space before installation and 8 or 16 for the TextHelp.

IBM has continuous speech dictation software called ViaVoice Gold. This product offers advanced speech recognition technology. It allows you to talk to the computer at a normal speaking rate, so that you can capture ideas and words by only saying them, the way you ordinarily would. You don't have to pause between words to allow the computer to keep up. It also features are a 22,000 word general vocabulary, an additional 64,000 word capability, and a ViaVoice playback feature that reads aloud exactly what you type on the screen. It adapts to you and actually learns from your corrections. It requires at least Windows 95, 166 MHz, Pentium processor, 125 MB free space, Creative Labs sound card, and a CD-ROM.

OTHER TECHNOLOGY

Sometimes, when you are in a hurry, you may not be able to use a computer. You may want to jot down a note, a message, or get the correct spelling of a word.

My Experience: If you're like me, you may write the note on the nearest piece of paper and then later be unable to read your handwriting. Taking a telephone message for my roommates was particularly frustrating. Often, the caller would not slow down and would have already hung up before I could ask him or her to repeat the message. I'd get the dates and times backwards and my roommates would have a hard time reading my handwriting. I became very unpopular as a message-taker. A gadget like the Language Master would have allowed me to punch in the message and store it correctly so that I could read it back to my roommate.

The Franklin Language Master 6000 Special Edition, a portable note taker and spellchecker, solves the problem. It features a PEACEbook picture communication binder with a LM-6000 Special Edition keyboard specifically developed for people with learning disabilities. Words and messages are read out loud, spelled out loud, or pronounced syllable by syllable. This device comes with headphones, batteries, and an AC adapter. A videotape is available on loan if you want more information on this piece of equipment. To order or to receive more information, contact TIGER Communication System, Inc. See the end of this chapter for the address and phone number.

A lot of other small accessories can help you get through your classes. For example, talking calculators can make that freshman algebra and those formulas in chemistry and physics go a bit easier.

My Experience: On a chemistry or physics test, I often would copy the wrong answer from my calculator. I copied what I saw, and it was usually backwards or scrambled. Sometimes I could convince a professor that I had done the problem right, but just copied the answer incorrectly from my calculator. Often, though, hard-nosed professors were worried about academic integrity and could not be convinced. A gadget like a talking calculator would have made all that unnecessary.

The TFi Eight Digit Talking Calculator is the answer to this problem. It can even come with an earphone so no one hears your answer but you. This calculator can be the regular math type or the scientific type for courses like chemistry or physics.

Talking equipment can be ordered from Technology for Independence, Inc. (TFi). See the end of this chapter for information on how to request a recent TFi catalog.

Another rather cool piece of technology is the Reading Pen by Sieko Instruments. I got to try this out at an educational conference as well. It was the coolest thing I had used to read with in a long time. I thought how many times I could have used this in a class when trying to read a handout that was given out during a lecture. Today I think WOW!, I could use this on a plane. This is a portable device that allows you to read whatever you want. You simply scan the word with the pen, it display the words on the pen's side on a digital screen. It will read the word out loud, (you can plug in earphones), and it will even define the word if you need it too. I have never seen this in stores but it can be ordered directly from Sieko Instruments. You can call 1-877-344-4040. The web site is also an option, www.readingpen.com. The last list price I saw was $300. But this may have gone down now. This is definitely worth a look!

Helpful Hints

I recommend that you do your research when looking for software and other technology to use in school. Find out the cost and find out if your college or university offers any of it. Be a smart shopper. Look for the best deal and the product that suits your needs.

You may be eligible for some form of reimbursement if you purchase adaptive technology. Locating the funds is time-consuming, however. You must be able to assess your own private resources and determine whether you meet the eligibility requirements for publicly funded programs. The National Rehabilitation Information Center (NARIC) has articles on obtaining and reimbursing adaptive equipment for people with disabilities, and can be a great source of information on money for adaptive equipment. NARIC's Funding Sources Checklist may help you find some ways to fund such purchases.

I also recommend ABLEDATA, a computerized clearinghouse of information about adaptive products that publishes a comprehensive list. Contact information appears at the end of this chapter.

One more resource for the purchase of adaptive equipment is a catalog called Closing the Gap. This resource directory is a guide to the selection of microcomputer technology for special education and rehabilitation. I've used this guide many times to get price information and descriptions of equipment both as a student and for my clients as a professional. Contact information is listed at the end of this chapter.

LESS EXPENSIVE STUDY AIDS

As this chapter on technology for the LD began to unfold, I realized how expensive LD technology is. Let's face it—the software and equipment I have talked about is pricey. And this is bad news if you are a struggling college student. Believe me, I know what it means to live on a student budget. I am still paying off college bills as I write this book. Pay attention to this next section. These are some technology tips that won't bankrupt you.

Tinted Overlays

This first item, found at any art store, is a piece of tinted plastic or overlay. Also referred to as a blocker, this device is simply placed over whatever piece of text you are reading. It helps me get much more out of what I am trying to learn because I can follow along with my text as I am listening to my tapes.

I first read about this technique in an article in the "Life" section of <u>USA Today</u>, on September 17, 1990. The title of the article was "Simple Treatment May Aid Dyslexics," and I did my best to decipher it. When I told a counselor (Betty W., wherever you are, thanks!) about it, she looked for this colored plastic, found it, and gave me a manila envelope full of red plastic overlays. The red ones work best for me, but other LD students I know like to use blue or green.

Once I started using this overlay I noticed my reading speed went up. Even times when I didn't have a tape of a book or an article to follow, my speed improved. And when I did have a tape, my reading and listening speeds both increased with the use of this very inexpensive tool.

Over the years I have read more about this technique, known as the Irlen method. These overlays are also referred to as Irlen filters, named for their founder Helen Irlen, an American educational psychologist, who presented a paper on them in August 1983, at the 91st Annual Convention of the American Psychological Association in Anaheim, California. Studies show that these filters work with some people with reading disabilities and that the readers do show results.

Although the way this technique works is rather complicated, I have found the best description on a website, www.irlenclinic.com. On this site, it states that "the tinted filters filter specific light frequencies and remove a range of perceptual disorders that adversely affect reading and related learning performance." These disorders are now known as Scotopic Sensitivity/Irlen Syndrome. The clinic states that you should be tested to see if these filters/overlays will work. If you do have Irlen Syndrome, a perceptual dysfunction, then you could find out other treatments. The information can be found at the end of this chapter. But I encourage you to try the filters on your own and see if it makes a difference.

A Specialized Optometrist

Another aid that can make a difference (and won't be as expensive as some of the other technologies I've discussed) is consulting a developmental optometrist. When I was in college, my vocational rehabilitation counselor (I will talk about the role of the vocational rehabilitation counselor in your life later) suggested that I see a developmental optometrist, an eye doctor whose specialty is working with people who have developmental reading disabilities.

My Experience: I needed prisms in my reading glasses to help with my reading. The way I understand it, the prisms help to defract the print from the paper and spread it over the retina in such a way that I can process it as one image.

Also, because I was a client of vocational rehabilitation, that agency paid for my first appointment and $100 on the glasses.

I highly recommend at least one visit to a developmental optometrist just to see if some kind of glasses can help you.

Inexpensive Technology

If you have trouble studying, an innovative desktop tool called STUDYMATE will help you. The best things about this software are that it is flexible and easy to use, and you can customize it to fit your needs. It can test you on the facts you need to know, based on your coursework; it can save and print study lists. It also scores and times your tests, and you can take these tests on the screen or on paper. All these features will help you memorize facts faster and easier and reduce your study time. This nifty piece of software is very inexpensive. You can get it from Jackson Software at 800-850-1777. The company may have other helpful devices, too, so ask for their catalogue. Another company that offers similar, inexpensive software is Compu-Teach, which can be found on the Internet at www.compu-teach.com.

RESNA

If you are not too sure about some of these technologies or if you want to stay aware of new and upcoming technology, I recommend that you join an organization called the Rehabilitation Engineering and Assistive Technology Society of North America (RESNA), an interdisciplinary association for the advancement of rehabilitation and assistive technologies. RESNA provides some very informative publications: the quarterly journal Assistive Technology, and RESNA News. You will probably be interested in the material under "special education," which covers information on assistive technology for the education of young people.

RESNA also maintains a public domain software library and an electronic bulletin board. As a student member of this organization you pay $50 for membership and the journal. For more information on this organization and a membership application, see the contact information at the end of this chapter.

Access to Computers at School

Most schools have computer labs available to all students. If you have not already discovered it for yourself, you will find that basic computer knowledge will make a huge difference in your life and in your learning. If you can afford your own computer, by all means buy one. You will be glad to have your own machine and not have to worry about computer availability in a crowded lab. It will be great to have your customized software on it as well.

Some DSS offices have computers with adaptive software on them. Check out the available adaptive equipment for LD students at all the colleges you are considering. Believe me, having the right equipment can make learning easier for you throughout your college years. The technology will not cure your learning disability, but it will increase your access to an equal education.

RESOURCES

Books on Tape and Accessories

American Printing House for the Blind
P. O. Box 6085
Louisville, KY 40206-0085
502/895-2405

Boston Information and Technology Corporation (BIT)
52 Roland Street
Boston, MA 02129
800/333-2481

National Library Service for the Blind and Physically Handicapped (NLS)
The Library of Congress
Washington, DC 20542
202/287-5927
(also inquire at your local library for borrowing information)

Recordings for the Blind and Dyslexic (RFB&D)
The Anne T. Macdonald Center
20 Roszel Road
Princeton, NJ 08540
800/803-7201

Computer Software Manufacturers and Distributors

Arkenstone
1-800-444-4443 or 650-603-8880
www.wynn.arkenstone.org

Computer Challenges-Satcom, Inc.
3400 International Drive, N.W.
Suite 2K-500
Washington, DC 20008
202/966-2555
Fax: 202/966-7393
ATTN: Carl H. Schmitt (President)
or Wallace P. Mack (Vice President)

Computeach
425/885-0517
www.compu-teach.com

Computernerdz
Computernerdz.com
Creative Labs
800/998-5227

Dragon Systems, Inc.
90 Bridge Street
Newton, MA 02158
617/985-5200
Fax: 617/527-0372

HumanWare, Inc.
6245 King Road
Loomis, CA 95650
916/652-7253 or
800/722-3393
916/652-7296 (Fax)

Jackson Software
800/850-1777

Lernout & Hauspre
800/894-5374
e-mail: education.info@LHSL.com

Seiko Instruments
877/344-4040
www.readingpen.com

TALKTYP
800/825-5897

Technology for Independence
529 Main Street
Boston, MA 02129
800/31-8255
Fax: 617/242-2007

Tiger Communication System, Inc.
Suite 325
155 East Broad Street
Rochester, NY 14604
716/454-5134 or
800/724-7301

Other Organizations

Center for IT Accommodation (CITA)
A nationally recognized model demonstration facility influencing accessible information environments, services, and management practices.
www.itpolicy.gsa.gov/cita/index.htm

Closing the Gap
A publication that highlights hardware and software products for persons with special needs.
www.closingthegap.com

Disability Resources
An on-line resource for Apple users. Great links and information.
www.apple.com/education/K12/disability.

Dyslexic.com
A great website for dyslexia and technology updates.
www.dyslexic.com/index.html
e-mail: sales@dyslexic.com

Irlen Clinic
Provides much information about Irlen Syndrome and Irlen filters.
www.irlenclinic.com
419/541-9566

Job Accommodation Network (JAN)
A toll-free consulting service that provides information about job accommodations and employability of people with disabilities. JAN also can provide information on the Americans with Disabilities Act (ADA).
800/526-7234
janweb.icdi.wvu.edu

RESNA
Suite 1540
1700 North Moore Street
Arlington, VA 22209-1903
703/524-6686 (Phone)
703/524-6630 (Fax)
703/524-6639 (TTY)
e-mail: info@resna.org

The Tinted Sky
A website dedicated to sharing information on Irlen Syndrome and filters.
www.interlog.com/%7Eandreab/smi/tts/go2.htm

Tools for Life
This organization is Georgia's assistive technology project and publishes A Closer Look, an assistive technology publication.
2 Peachtree St., Suite 35-415
Atlanta, GA 30303
800/497-8665
404/657-3084

Books

Hogging, K. & Boone, R. (Eds.). (1997). <u>Technology for Students with Learning Disabilities</u>. Austin, TX: PRO-ED, Inc.

CHAPTER 7:
MANAGING YOUR TIME

Lots of college students have problems budgeting their time, but the learning disabled find it especially hard to judge time well. They usually are not good estimators of a block of time—how long it will take to get something done or to go somewhere. It is very common for learning disabled students to be very early for a class or very late. They seem to have trouble grasping the distance from point A to point B and the time it will take to get there. To avoid over- or underestimating time, you will need to walk from your dorm or apartment to find out just how long it will take to get to your class or to take public transportation. Then you need to budget that traveling time into your everyday life.

Knowing how to manage your time is a skill. In fact, mastering this skill gives you the ability to **schedule** time, which in turn helps you **gain** time. Here are some things I have done that helped me manage my time well.

One thing that helped me organize my time was writing down all the things I did in one day and how much time it took to do them. It certainly made me realize that the amount of time I was spending studying for an upcoming exam was not nearly as much as I thought. I was also amazed at how long I took in the morning to drink a cup of coffee and get ready for the day. I also discovered that I had about two extra hours in the day that I didn't know about. I was using up too much time getting from my last class of the day to the subway because I spent a lot of it window-shopping and talking to my friends. I found a whole extra hour for studying if I walked straight to the subway and went home. By analyzing how you spend each day, you may find that the time you need is probably there. You just need to find it and put it to good use.

Thinking of time in small blocks was something I also found helpful and much easier to grasp. Scheduling your day this way does not mean that you will never have free time. When you make up your schedule, you can plan your own free time. And when you begin to follow a structured timetable, you may find the free time you never thought you had. But don't forget the obvious things—like sleeping and eating.

I will give you an example of a chart I use to help me keep my days and even my hours organized.

THE LD CALENDAR

This calendar has been a survival tool for me. I developed it slowly, as I learned from my mistakes and found what worked for me and what didn't. The syllabus that most professors give you on the first day of class will help you to turn your calendar into your own map for daily living and learning.

Let's review this calendar. First, notice the large amount of space for each hour. This calendar is not meant to be pocket-sized, something that you can just slip into your jeans and carry around with you. It is meant to be notebook sized. Notice, too, that the calendar reads in blocks of time and begins at 7:00 A.M. You can fill in days and dates at the top of the page, so you won't be writing in the wrong activities or classes on the wrong day. I prefer to write the days of the week in red, but when you personalize the calendar, choose the color that's best for you. I highlight the times on mine in green, the color I found the clearest and most comfortable to read, next to the red dates and days. If you use a tinted overlay on the calendar, remember to use a different color pen or what you write will not show through. I recommend you copy the calendar, three-hole punch it, and then put it in a notebook.

When you open up the calendar pages to a day, you will see 7:00 A.M.–8:00 P.M. facing you. This setup allows you to see the whole day at one glance without having to turn the pages. The evening sheet on the next page starts with a block at 9:00 P.M. and continues to midnight.

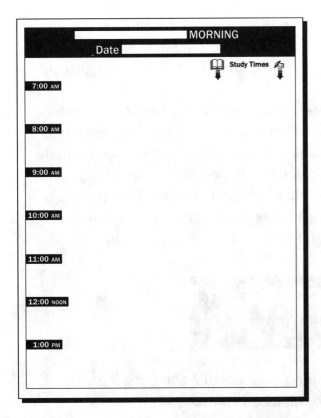

MORNING

Date

📖 Study Times ✍

7:00 AM

8:00 AM

9:00 AM

10:00 AM

11:00 AM

12:00 NOON

1:00 PM

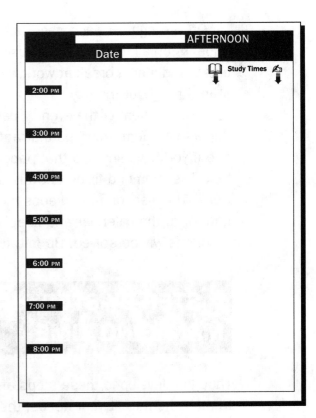

AFTERNOON

Date

📖 Study Times ✍

2:00 PM

3:00 PM

4:00 PM

5:00 PM

6:00 PM

7:00 PM

8:00 PM

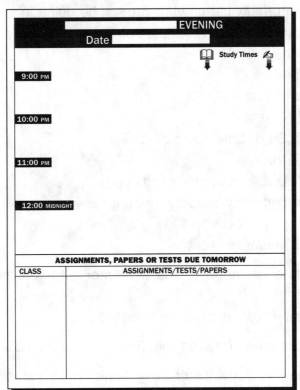

EVENING

Date

📖 Study Times ✍

9:00 PM

10:00 PM

11:00 PM

12:00 MIDNIGHT

ASSIGNMENTS, PAPERS OR TESTS DUE TOMORROW	
CLASS	ASSIGNMENTS/TESTS/PAPERS

On the right of each page is a column for your study times. This column appears on all the pages because any time is a good time to study—between classes, during a break at work, while you are eating. These are times you can fit in throughout the day.

At the bottom of the evening page is a section labeled "Assignments/Tests/ Papers Due Tomorrow" so that at the end of each day you can look down and see if you have finished that paper, done that assignment, or studied for that test. I recommend filling out this section for each day at the beginning of the week. This section really keeps me on top of things and on my toes. If you are faithful to the calendar and keep it up to date, then half of your organization problems will be solved. Be faithful to it and it will be faithful to you.

A STEP-BY-STEP PROCESS FOR MANAGING TIME

Though I developed these steps after many years of trial and error, if you need to alter them to fit your needs, then by all means do so.

Step 1: Make a priority list of what you will be doing in school this semester. For example, Priority 1 should be classes. Priority 2 is study time, and so forth.
Example:
Priority List
1. Classes
2. Study time/tutor time
3. Job
4. Leisure time for sanity
5. Fraternity/sorority meetings, events, sports or other extracurricular activities
6. Volunteer work

Step 2: Set up a calendar for the semester with your courses and course times.
In other words, expand on Priority 1.

Step 3: Add your times for studying, Priority 2, to the calendar

Step 4: Include your activities or obligations on the calendar

This section is for things other than courses (such as work), or the next priorities you have listed. Continue until you have the whole list on your calendar. You may find that you have to drop some activities to have the time to study and meet with a tutor to get through the semester. To finish my undergraduate and graduate work, I had to cut back on much of my social time. I had to miss many of the events at my school and make some difficult choices about what was important to me.

A Few Tips for Making up Your Time Schedule:

- ✎ Take advantage of any kind of college orientation before you start your freshman year. In addition, go on a walking tour to help you get familiar with the campus.

- ✎ Plan to do your study time as soon after your classes as possible, as well as during other times, such as waiting for a bus or subway.

- ✎ Schedule study time in 50-minute blocks with 10-to-15 minute breaks or what is the best time for you.

- ✎ Use the list of priorities that you developed to remind you of what you need to be working on.

- ✎ Plan for travel time to and from classes.

CHAPTER 8:

JOY'S TIPS FOR LEARNING HOW TO LEARN

This chapter will probably be the most valuable for you. Many topics will be discussed here, from scheduling your classes and registering for them, to getting organized to write a paper. Some of the things that work for me may not work for you. For example, I use color-coding in organizing my papers as well as in my everyday life. If you're color blind, though, that technique is obviously not going to work for you. I urge you to try my strategies if you don't yet have methods of your own, however. You can always adapt them to work for you.

GETTING STARTED FOR THE SEMESTER: REGISTERING FOR CLASSES

Obviously, your first task is to register for your classes. Registration can be a nightmare. Some colleges have you register for your first classes by mail. If you have this option, be sure that someone looks over your registration form and checks that you have written down the codes correctly. You may have reversed numbers and letters and then find yourself registered for classes you've never heard of.

If registration is done electronically by phone, be sure that you punch in the numbers correctly. Sometimes it may take two or three calls to get your whole schedule punched in correctly, especially if you're reading numbers incorrectly and cannot find your mistake. You may be better off going to the Disabled Students Services office and asking one of the staff to punch the numbers in for you. You might also get help from your roommate, if you feel comfortable doing that.

My Experience: My history of attempting to register for classes is marked by many strikeouts. As an undergraduate, I often made mistakes on my registration form. I would copy numbers incorrectly from the semester schedule and/or write the name of the course on the wrong line. At times I even wrote my social security number down wrong by reversing some of the numbers.

Toward the end of my long undergraduate career, when the university I was attending switched to electronic phone registration, I thought the process would be easier for me. After all, I wouldn't have to write. But when I got on that phone and tried to read the numbers off the registration form and then punch them into the system, I was overwhelmed. It was especially hard since I had to do it within a limited amount of time, or I'd have to start all over again.

I finally decided I was going to ask for help registering, so I went to the Disabled Student Services office. They were glad to help me register correctly. I continued to go there to have them do the number punching throughout school. I was amazed at how fast the process can be if you ask for help.

TIPS ON SCHEDULING CLASSES

Here are some tips to help you schedule your classes:

- ✎ Do not schedule more classes than you think you can handle in one day. Too much information all at once may overwhelm you.

- ✎ Try to sit in on a class before you register for it.

- ✎ Register for at least one class each semester in a subject area you find interesting and enjoyable.

TALKING WITH YOUR PROFESSORS

Going to see professors before the class begins will put you ahead of the game. If you are not sure how to break the ice with the professor, then check to see if your DSS will send a letter to the professor before you meet. This letter could explain your learning disability and the accommodations you might find helpful. Ask to see the letter before it is sent because it **cannot** be sent without your permission.

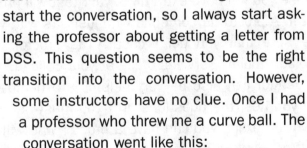

My Experience: I have always appreciated having a letter sent to my professors before the first day of class. I can never think of the right words to start the conversation, so I always start asking the professor about getting a letter from DSS. This question seems to be the right transition into the conversation. However, some instructors have no clue. Once I had a professor who threw me a curve ball. The conversation went like this:

Joy: "Did you get a letter from DSS regarding an LD student? I'm that student."

Physics Professor: "What's LD?"

Needless to say, I was taken aback, but I went on to explain what it was, and he finally recalled a letter he received. So even though the meeting doesn't always go just the way you plan, I find the letter to be really helpful in breaking down that first barrier between an LD student and professor.

TAKING EXAMS

Test-taking challenges can vary, depending on the course and the test taker. Your ability to use the methods that I will be discussing will also depend on the support services and resources at your school. But always remember that you have the right to any reasonable accommodations. Several kinds of accommodations can be helpful when you are taking an exam. I urge you to explore all of them and use the ones that best fit your needs and your way of learning.

The first thing to consider is that when you take exams outside of the classroom (i.e., in a room or building different from the one where the class is taking the exam), then the instructor won't be available for questions during the exam. Therefore, meeting and going over the test with the professor should be part of your preparation.

Because you will be taking the exam in a testing room or private office and because you will have extra time, your test will probably be administered by a **proctor.** A proctor is someone who just sits with you while you take a test to make sure that you don't cheat. The proctor is usually provided by the Disabled Student Services office at your college.

A **reader** can also be very helpful in a number of ways. If you do better when you hear the questions or if you must hear as well as follow along on the written exam, you can have a proctor who will read the test questions to you. If so, you will probably be taking the exam in a private testing room so that you don't disturb the rest of the class.

Some professors prefer to read the exam to you themselves, however. Some may even want to read the exam quietly to you in the same room where the class is taking the exam and at the same time. If you don't feel comfortable with this arrangement, let the professor know that having the exam read to you in view of the rest of the class infringes on your right to confidentiality concerning your disability. If the professor insists on being the one to read to you, then you should insist on taking the test in privacy and either before or after the class takes it.

Scribes help you write the answer down on the exam and, again, this scribe could also be the proctor and reader as well. Many times a professor will suggest a scribe to you if your handwriting is as atrocious as mine. All you do is tell the scribe what to write. This method also helps because you can say the answer out loud and talk yourself through the exam by hearing what you are thinking and utilizing the verbal skills at which LD students are often better. Always have the scribe read the answer back to you. This allows you to hear again out loud the answer you gave and to make sure he or she wrote what you said.

PCs are also a great idea and a PC with SoundProof or some other adaptive screen device or voice activated software on it is even better. With it, you don't have to write and can print up your legible answers to the test immediately after. You may still need someone to read the questions and directions to you. In addition, you should find out if you can run a spell check and/or a grammar program through your answers. Some professors think that somehow answers appear magically on the screen for you, so they won't allow you to use them. But remember you have a right to whatever reasonable accommodations you need. The definition of "necessary and reasonable" may vary with professors and colleges, so you should ask questions about them before you decide to attend the school.

Oral exams can be another option for those of us who prefer talking through the exam, rather than writing it. This method could work a few different ways. You could have someone read the questions, then you would dictate your answers onto audio tape. After the exam, depending the professor's preference, the office for disabled student services or the professor can transcribe the tape. This type of test taking seems to work really well for those long essay exams.

Another possibility is taking a test orally with the professor. It can be nerve-wracking to tell your answers directly to the instructor, but you don't have to worry about being taped. Only twice in my seven-year undergraduate career did I take an exam this way. The advantage here is really only for the professor, who can usually at once whether you studied and know the material and can grade you immediately.

Untimed exams are a given for the student with a learning disability. No matter which of these styles of taking exams you prefer, you should always get double, if not unlimited time to finish an exam. The untimed exam puts no stress on you for a speedy finish. With double time, either you or the proctor still has to keep an eye on the clock. Many times a professor will offer double time just because it's the least that they can do and follow the law. If you are offered only double time, however, and you feel that you need an untimed exam, then by all means fight for it. Explain that processing takes much more time for you than for the average person, as you have to decode and unscramble the information on the test. Let it be known that when you hear the question or read the question, often times you must hear it or read it a second or third time just to understand it or process it in the right order. By no means does this accommodation interfere with the academic integrity of the class or the college or university.

Many of these functions, like proctoring or reading, can be combined. For example, your reader can act as a proctor and as a scribe. So providing these accommodations is really not a huge expense for a school. Many of the people that do such jobs are the work-study students, who are glad to have a paid job. Of course, if they are being paid by the hour, they prefer that you have ALL the time you need to complete an exam.

WRITING A PAPER: MY COLOR-CODED METHOD

The research paper tends to fill lots of college students with dread. They're afraid to do it and tend to procrastinate about working on it. However, I have a color-coded system that can eliminate some of the grief of organizing and completing this assignment. I call it the color-coded system because I use colored index cards to organize the paper. Here are the steps:

Step 1: Talk to your Professor

The first step is to discuss possible topics with your professor. Since identifying a topic can be difficult, use your instructor to get suggestions but be sure to pick a topic that interests you.

You may need some help researching this topic, so using your professor as a resource is a good idea. You should have some topics in mind when you meet with your professor. Then you can narrow them down to the one your instructor thinks might best fit the assignment.

Keep in mind that the university library is not your only resource. Your school may have a library consortium program that enables you to use books and periodicals from other school libraries. Furthermore, most libraries are connected to a whole network of information via computer. And you have all those sources on the Internet to choose from, too.

Step 2: Find Your References

Once you have a clear idea of what you're going to write about, go to the library and begin to look for references by doing a subject search on your topic. You can do this at your college library through the online computer system. Ask the reference librarians for help using these programs.

Don't try to get too many references at one time. Locate about 10 sources and pick the ones most relevant to your subject. This method will help you narrow down to a specific topic. (Remember to use adaptive equipment like the Kurzweil Reader or a tutor to get through your references.) Then locate 10 more sources and keep narrowing those down until you think you have enough to complete your paper. That's all for one day. Take a break and come back to it the next day.

Step 3: Develop an Outline

An outline, if done correctly, can be a real asset to the writing of your paper. Once you've developed an outline, you've basically written the paper. All you need to do afterward is to fill in any gaps with information from your sources.

The best help for developing an outline is the table of contents from a book on your subject. This page divides the material covered in the book into chapter titles; from these titles you can create entries for your outline.

What follows is an outline based on a paper I wrote on the psychosocial aspects and adjustments for persons with learning disabilities. If you've never done an outline before, you alternate between numbers and letters to organize it, starting by designating the broadest sections as Roman numerals I, II, III, etc. You then subdivide each Roman numeral into capital letters A, B, C, and so forth until you've covered all your subdivisions for that Roman numeral. Each capital letter gets divided into numbers 1, 2,and so on, and each regular number gets divided into small letters a, b, c, etc. The main thing to remember is that you only need to subdivide a section when you have more than one topic to address in that section. In other words, you cannot have a I if you don't eventually expect to have a II; you don't need to create an A if you don't have a B, or a 1 if you don't have a 2.

Although my outline may seem long, it was developed for a graduate-level paper, so I had to make it thorough. Your outline may not be as long or have as many divisions. But it is important that you do an outline correctly—when you have developed a good outline, you will be ready to write your paper.

From here, you're ready to start the color coding. But first take a break.

(Correct outline format)

Psychosocial Aspects and Adjustments for Persons with Learning Disabilities

I. The learning disability
    A. Definition and statistics
    B. Types of learning disabilities
        1. Dyslexia
        2. Dysgraphia
        3. Dyscalcula
        4. Attention-Deficit Disorder(ADD) and Attention-Deficit Hyperactive Disorder(ADHD)
    C. Associated characteristics
        1. Seizure disorder
        2. Motor coordination disorders
            a. Perceptual-motor disorder
            b. Visual-motor disorder
            c. Auditory-motor disorder

---

3. Perceptual disorders
    a. Auditory-perceptual disorders
    b. Proprioceptive disorder
    c. Tactile-perceptual disorder
    d. Visual-perceptual disorder
    e. Vestibular-perceptual disorder
4. Intersensory problems
5. Memory problems
6. Soft neurological disorders

II. Assessing and diagnosing the person with a learning disability
    A. Screening and diagnosing techniques and measurements
        1. Basic psycho-educational tests
        2. Other screening techniques
    B. Physical exam
        1. Neurological exam
        2. Behavior assessment
        3. Optical exam

III. Social adjustments of the person with a learning disability
    A. The nonvisible disability
        B. Social status
        1. Acceptance by peers
        2. Social cognition deficits (socially tone deaf) and specific brain hemispheres
            a. Social competencies
            b. Children and adjustment problems
    C. Behavior issues
        1. School avoidance
        2. Homework avoidance
        3. Television addiction
        4. Cheating
        5. Aggression
        6. Controlling behavior

(continued next page)

(continued from previous page)

       7. Quitting

       8. Withdrawal

    D. Family issues

IV. Psychological and emotional adjustments of the person with a learning disability

    A. Emotional issues

       1. Self-esteem

       2. Depression and suicide

    B. Personality issues

    C. Drug and alcohol abuse

V. Treatment

    A. Learning compensations

    B. Developmental optometrists

    C. Special education programs

       1. Within the public school system

       2. Special/special schools

VI. Learning disabled adults

    A. Employment issues

       1. Protection under the American with Disabilities Act

       2. Disclosure

    B. Social issues

    C. Further education

VII. Implications for the field of vocational rehabilitation and the client with a learning disability

    A. Perceptions of learning disabilities

    B. Learning disabilities and vocational rehabilitation

    C. Self-advocacy

    D. Role models

Step 4: Color Code Your Cards

Once you have a good outline, go back to those sources that you identified and begin finding the information for each section. Assign a color to each Roman numeral division (I, II, III, etc.). Put each bit of information you find on the corresponding colored card.

      I. = white
      II. = blue
      III. = orange

If you can find only white index cards, put a colored dot in the corner of the card with a marker to correspond with the assigned color.

Now you should have index cards of different colors that represent the main sections of your outline (and your paper). Next, put the cards in an envelope or index cardholder. Label this file with a Roman numeral—I or whatever section you're working on. Because the cards are color coded, you will be able to keep them separate. Now take a break.

Step 5: Record More Specific Information

Since an outline gets more specific as you further divide a subject, the next set of cards (A, B, C, etc.) will be a little more specific than the ones for I, II, III, and so on. These will be color-coded the same way as the Roman numeral division cards. For example, if I is white, then IA should be white, too. When you have gone through your references and completed these cards, put them in an envelope and label it with the letter of that division.

After that, you can repeat this process for the next level (1, 2, 3 . . .) and label the envelope "Number 1 information cards."

Repeat the procedure again for the cards with lower-case letters (a, b, c, etc.). Put these in an envelope and label it the same way you did the others. Then you can take a break.

Step 6: Bring All the Pieces Together

At this point, you have gone through your outline and made information cards for every division. For this step you will need a lot of space to spread out all the cards. Begin by opening each envelope, starting with the ones with

Roman numerals. Then place the contents of each envelope in a line. Next place the upper-case lettered cards next to the corresponding Roman numeral. Continue this process until you have gone through all the envelopes.

Now you should have a very long line of index cards laid out in the order of your outline. This line may stretch out across your bedroom floor or all the way across a dorm hallway, depending on how comprehensive your paper is. But no matter how long it is, you should realize that you just organized a lot of information in an orderly fashion. So you deserve a long break. (You don't have to leave all the cards on the floor. You can number them and store them in a file box.)

Step 7: Write the Paper

Now you are ready to shape all this information into a well-structured paper. Going card by card, in the order of your outline, write out the information from the cards.

Then take a break.

Step 8: Proofread

Always have an objective person with good writing skills, such as the LD specialist at your school, proofread your paper. Ask that person to read it twice to make sure that the content is easy to follow and that it has no typographical errors. Even today at my job, I have colleagues proofread everything I write. It really makes a difference.

Just a few reminders:

- Always take advantage of the adaptive equipment available at your school.

- Ask tutors or notetakers to help you in the library.

- Take as many breaks as you need, even if it is in the middle of a step.

That's my system, and it has worked well for me. But remember, this is a process I discovered that suited the way that I process information. Try it yourself—but don't hesitate to adapt the color-coded method so that it works for you.

TAKING SUMMER COURSES

If you decide to take courses in the summer sessions, you really should know what you're getting into. Summer classes are usually much more accelerated and therefore are harder to keep up with. But not all learning disabled people have problems succeeding in a summer class.

There are many reasons why you may want to take a summer course. For example, you may have failed a course and want to retake it in the summer to be able to graduate on time. Another reason may be to try to finish college a little sooner than your current pace would allow. These are legitimate reasons; however, you should prepare yourself. The following tips should be helpful:

- Talk to the professor who is teaching the course beforehand. This may be difficult, because many times adjunct professors who are not at the university full-time teach the summer courses. But if you go to the department office, you can probably get the professor's telephone number or leave yours.

- Ask questions about the reading load for the class, the number of papers required, the type of exams given, and the length of the term. Summer courses can last anywhere from four to eight weeks.

- Tell the professor that you have a learning disability and ask if he or she has ever had an LD student in the summer class before.

- Check with your Disabled Student Services office at your school and be sure they know you will be taking a class (or classes). You should also find out if readers and note takers are available for the summer sessions.

- Check to see if you can take the course at a community college and transfer the credit. The benefit is that you may be able to go to your hometown to take the class at the local community college. You may also be able to get more one-to-one attention. If you choose this option, however, be sure that you check with the equivalent department at your full-time college to ensure that they will give you credit for classes you take at another school. The department may wish to see the syllabus or the texts for the course you intend to take, so plan ahead! It is often much more difficult to get approval for courses you've taken at another school after you have taken them.

USING THE STRATEGY PROGRAM

Here are some of my general classroom strategies for success. I think you may find them helpful.

Sit in on a class before you take it.

Tape all lectures.

Review the tapes and transcribe them (or have them transcribed) **as soon after class as possible.**

Arrange in advance for test accommodations and use of adaptive equipment and adaptive methods.

Tutors: get them and use them. (Preferably tutors who have worked with learning disabled students before.

Every course should be reviewed every day or every other day. Keeping up with the class is vital!

Gauge your time so that you have plenty for studying.

Your own way of learning will help you to succeed.

S **Sitting** in on a class before you register for it is a very wise move. For example, let's say you want to take a chemistry class. If you sit in on it first, you will be able to see how fast the professor talks or how quickly he or she writes things on the board and then erases them. Visiting a class is easy to arrange. All you have to do is go to the professor ahead of time and explain that you are a learning disabled student who is interested in taking the class, but that you want to see if you can handle it before you register. You don't have to identify yourself as a student with a learning disability if you don't want to. You can just be an interested student thinking of taking the class.

Of course, you will have required courses that you have no choice but to take. You will have some flexibility in your electives and your major, however.

So when you choose those courses, think back on your testing and the recommendations made to you. Try to emphasize your strengths when you make these decisions. For example, if you have strong verbal skills or if you learn better verbally, why not try a speech class?

T **Taping** all your lectures can be very helpful. For one thing, it is good backup in case your note taker misses something or is absent. Also, taping is invaluable for someone who learns best by repetition. However, as the next tip suggests, playing and replaying your lecture tapes will be of greatest benefit to you if you listen to the tape and study your notes as soon after class as possible.

R **Reviewing** your tapes right after class will help you remember the material. Your learning disability may make it hard for you to remember information, so before you forget what the class was about, you should listen to that tape.

If you need two modes of input (visual and auditory) to understand what you are reading or listening to, you should have your tapes transcribed. If a reader does your text reading, that person can usually transcribe tapes for you. If not, check with the school's office for disabled student services (or the office that provides services to you), to find out if they can help you make arrangements. Of course, if you can, transcribe the tapes yourself. You may find that the process of transcription helps you learn the information.

Another form of review I found helpful was something I call conversational learning, something you can do with a study partner or even a tutor. The activity has no special format: you just involve yourself in stimulating discussion about the subject. For example, if you are studying for a religion exam and one of the topics is Catholicism, talking about the power of the Pope or the top three controversies in that religion can help you become familiar with the major focuses of this religion. Then, when you take the essay test, you may remember the words used in that conversation.

A **Accommodations** on tests can vary for each person, and you will need to **arrange** for them in advance. When I was in college, for each exam I had a reader who read me the questions and also wrote down my answers, because most professors found my handwriting very difficult to read. Sometimes a professor would allow me to dictate my answers into a tape recorder. In those cases, the reader only had to read the questions, and then I would put my answers onto the tape. Some professors, however, found it inconvenient to have to listen to a tape. If so, the Office for Disabled Student Services would transcribe the tape before it went to the professor.

T **Tutors** should become a part of your life in college if you are having trouble in a particular area of study. The key is to find a tutor who has worked with people with learning disabilities. The staff at your school's office for disabled student services may be able to recommend an experienced tutor. You may also want to go to the school's education department to find a student in the reading, special education, or teacher training programs who is interested in tutoring. In most of these programs, students work with someone who is learning disabled to fulfill a requirement of their degree.

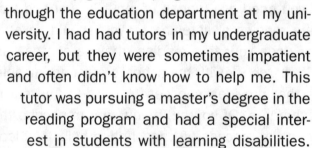

My Experience: I had a wonderful tutor in the first semester of my graduate program, whom I found through the education department at my university. I had had tutors in my undergraduate career, but they were sometimes impatient and often didn't know how to help me. This tutor was pursuing a master's degree in the reading program and had a special interest in students with learning disabilities. She had tricks to help me broaden my vocabulary, and was a tremendous asset when it came to the grammatical stuff in my papers. My only regret was that I didn't meet her when I was an undergraduate student.

E **Every day** (or every other day) was my rule for reviewing each course. I found that if I started slacking off and I let a course get ahead of me, I would hardly ever catch up. While some people can open a book only in the classroom and still do well on an exam, as a learning disabled person, I am not one of them. I had to work twice as hard to get the same results as other students. It was frustrating, but it was and is still a reality. I know from hard experience that you have to review at least a portion of your notes and tapes from a class and to do it **every day!** Don't get behind!

G **Gauging** your time is a skill you must master. Estimating time is one thing that people with learning disabilities do not do well. A learning disabled student may guess that some task will take an hour, and two hours later she still thinks she has time left over. Frequently, a person with a learning disability will underestimate the time it will take to get from one place to another. Other times, an LD student will plan on finishing something, but before long, the day is gone and he never even started on that paper. Clearly, gauging time correctly is an asset.

I find it helpful to think in blocks of time and use a color-coded calendar (more on this technique later in this chapter). One thing you can do is to keep an extra watch in your book bag or tape one to your planner. This practice worked for me on those days when I forgot to wear a watch.

Y The **"YOU"** rule is the last and most important one in my philosophy of learning. The best way to describe what you do in an academic setting (and what you will be doing for the rest of your life) is **learning how to learn.** It is true that because we are learning disabled, we do not succeed as well as others in a traditional learning setting. So, whatever methods you find that help you succeed, use them and stick with them! You must figure out how **you** learn best.

CHAPTER 9:

SUPPORT AND HINTS FOR GENERAL LIVING

SUPPORT

Your emotional well-being is extremely important. It's likely that from time to time, you'll need support from sources outside of yourself, so it will be help know where to go for that help. There is a list of resources at the end of this chapter that may assist you. If some of these organizations are not in the area where you are going to school, then call any of the national or international organizations for a local listing of resources or support groups.

First and foremost, however, be aware of the groups that can be helpful right on campus. For example, your school may have a learning disability resource group or support group. You may want to ask at the Disabled Student Services office or the department that provides your services and accommodations to find out what is available on campus and in the area.

A **support group** may be an informal gathering where LD students get together and just listen to each other. It really helps to talk to someone who knows what you are dealing with every day. You can also hear the horror stories of "fellow sufferers." This exchange can be helpful in identifying the professors and the classes to avoid. If there is not a support group on campus, then go to the disabled student services office and tell them you want to start one. It will really make a difference in your life. At times you will need to vent to those who will best understand exactly what you are going through. Use the help of those disabled students around you.

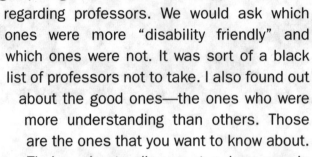

My Experience: When I was in college I helped start a support group on campus. We would use the group to get information from upper-classmen regarding professors. We would ask which ones were more "disability friendly" and which ones were not. It was sort of a black list of professors not to take. I also found out about the good ones—the ones who were more understanding than others. Those are the ones that you want to know about. Their understanding went a long way in helping me get my degrees. If at all possible, avoid the ones who have given other LD students a hard time. If you can't avoid taking someone you have been warned about, talk to your DSS representative, who probably knows about the professor. Knowing that you have support from that office can help you start the class with a positive attitude and keep it when you encounter a problem. Sometimes your representative can act as a moderator in sticky situations. Always try to work them out, and never burn your bridges—you may have to work with that professor again. Besides the letter that DSS writes, a good way to begin is to let the instructor know that you are taping the class. That way you show respect for the way he or she conducts the course.

The support group was also a source for tips on studying and just getting through college. The group helped to create a network of support in college when I was away from home. It really meant a lot to me and, even today, those people in that original group are still my close friends.

A **resource group,** by contrast, is one that schedules speakers and workshops. More of an informational group than the support group, the resource group may be especially helpful to the LD college student who is not aware of certain services, technology, and other things that will help make the semester a little bit easier. Some groups may also combine resources and support.

The **career center** is another good resource. They may offer informative speakers or workshops.

Frequently, the career center on campus has support groups, as well.

Within the college, your **academic advisor** can be a valuable resource. Use this person for advice on your class schedule. You should also be aware that your **advisor at Disabled Students Services** or your **learning disabilities specialist** may act as a liaison between you and your academic advisor, especially if your advisor has not worked with a student who has a learning disability before.

If you find yourself becoming overwhelmed or depressed, another person who can help is a **counselor.** Consult your college counseling center for a referral. Counseling can be an essential part of your semester. Don't hesitate to use this service if you need to.

My Experience: I have been and always will be an advocate of counseling. At times I was overwhelmed by frustrations with school, on top of other events in my life, and seeing a mental health professional was the solution for me. The process worked, and I got through some hard times. I realized that I had put in too much work to let some emotional issues go unattended and ruin my chances of accomplishing my goals.

If you are on medication for ADHD, then continue to communicate with your physician. This communication is imperative, because your medication doses may need to be adjusted from time to time.

THE VOCATIONAL REHABILITATION COUNSELOR

This counselor is one of the best resources I can give you. As a disabled person, you are entitled to the services offered by your state vocational rehabilitation services. These are the offices in every state that offer vocational rehabilitation services to persons with disabilities. If you have an IEP in place in your school now, then chances are that you have had a vocational rehabilitation counselor on your IEP transition team since your junior year in high school.

The office of vocational rehabilitation services offers a variety of services to disabled person, including assessment, diagnostic services, vocational training, job placement, and expenses paid for certain accommodation items as long that accommodation will lead to gainful employment. Career counseling and vocational evaluation are also provided, if needed. Some states have vocational rehabilitation centers that allow clients to try different types of assistive technology. And all of these services are FREE. This program has helped put disabled persons into training and work since 1973.

If you do not have a vocational counselor on your IEP team, then you should make an appointment with your local vocational rehabilitation office and get in the system. You can find them listed under the government pages in your local phone book. Your school may also assist you in getting registered. If you are already planning to go away to college, you should register with your vocational rehabilitation office in your residing state. Your assigned vocational counselor will help you prepare for this very important transition to college. You will determine your counselor's level of involvement.

Once you go there, all of your current documentation will be assessed, but you may be asked to take more tests and get more assessments conducted. If you have enough and you are found to be eligible for services, then you will begin working on an "individual employment plan" because the goal of the vocational rehabilitation counselor is getting you placed in substantial gainful employment. This plan will include the steps that it takes to get you to the goal. For example, if your goal is to become a speech therapist and you will need a bachelor's degree to reach that goal, then that degree is what vocational rehabilitation will pay for. Your college degree is the training you need to reach your stated employment goal. Getting a client placed is referred to in the vocational rehabilitation field as "getting a 26."

My Experience: I finally registered with vocational rehabilitation after I had already spent a few years in college. I found out about it from another student I met who told me that her state VR was paying for her tuition services. In my case, the VR covered more testing because I had a few other medical issues directly related to my disability. They also paid for the developmental optometrist who provided me with eye training and a pair of special glasses to help me read. They also covered my medication. All of these elements were impairment-related expenses that I needed to reach my stated employment goal. As long as everything was directly related to my goal, it was considered a reasonable expense.

The vocational rehabilitation counselor is going to be one the best supports that you can have as you work towards your stated goal.

GENERAL LIVING TIPS

Since life in general gives me headaches, I find that the less complicated I make my life, the better off I am. For example, I have problems with money. Figuring how much change I should get back after I make a purchase has always been hard for me. I had to find a way to avoid this headache, at least some of the time. The answer was the meal card that most colleges have. At the  beginning of each month, you put the amount of money you think you'll need to pay for food on the card. This way, the amount you spend for each meal is subtracted from the card. You have no charge to worry about paying for, just the card. Presto, here was one less headache!

Another major headache I had with money was reconciling my account at the end of the month because the columns are so small, and I had a hard time staying in the columns in the checkbook register. My solution was to use color-coding with my checking account. There are several ways to do this, so you need to find what works for you. I color-code the spending/withdrawals and the deposits. All money coming in is in GREEN. All money going out is in RED. I also write the monthly bills that come up every month in BLUE. At a glance, if I am trying to find more money for spending, I know right away because I can see the minimum for bills that I need each month.

Another obvious tip is time management control. Use the LD calendar. It will make all the difference in the world. Make a schedule that allows for study time and leisure time. Make room for upcoming papers and the research time you will need to get them done. If you block the time into your calendar then you are more likely to make sure you get it done. You must have complete control over your own time. If you do not, then it will take control of you. USE THE CALENDAR! It will make a difference. Time management should also allow for a social life—well, some social life. Be sure to be good to yourself in this regard, but not too good.

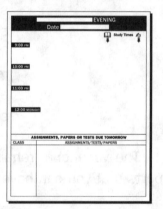

Your living environment will be very important to your success. Be prepared for those roommates who are not easy to study around and who don't have time management skills that allow you the study time that you need. It will be up to you to be assertive and make it clear that you need some quiet time and a quiet place where you can study if your own room is a problem.

Know your disability. Know all about your strengths and challenges. Know how to describe your disability to everyone who needs to know about it to make your college experience a successful one.

Educate, advocate, and disclose are the three rules to live by. If you do not educate people about your disability, no one else will. If you do not advocate for yourself, there will be days when no one else will. If you do not disclose, then no one will know that you need accommodations. The college or university administrators and the professors are not mind readers. You must be able to ask for what you need, and therefore, you must disclose what your challenges are.

Know what your needs are before you make your final choice for school. If the college is not right for you, you should know it before you start going to classes. Knowing what you need involves asking the right questions. A good college or university match is very important to a successful college career. The technology that assists your learning process, the level of acceptance of your learning differences, and the college support of your educational goals are the TLC's of that success.

Use this book as a guide for creating your own strategies and survival methods. You can be and accomplish anything you want to. There are learning disabled professionals all over the world in every profession imaginable. Don't settle on the field or career that is an easy way out. You will always be Learning How to Learn no matter what path you choose. Good is not enough when you dream of being great!

AFTERWORD

Please let me hear about your experiences. I really do want to find out about your learning disability and your college experience. Anything that you find useful may be useful to others. Please send your comments, stories, and tips to:

Learning How to Learn
147 North French Street
Alexandria, VA 22304

Or Fax: 703-823-8349

Or E-Mail: Joycobb1@juno.com

CHECKLIST OF QUESTIONS TO ASK AT COLLEGES AND UNIVERSITIES

College _____ **Telephone** _____

Contact person _____

QUESTIONS TO ASK	YES	NO
Does this college or university have a learning disabilities program, or does it provide services for the learning disabled under general disabled services? — Learning disability program or structured program — Learning disability services		
If the college or university has a separate LD program, do I need to apply to that program as well as to the college?		
What does the college or university require for proof of documentation? _____		
Does the college or university have an added fee for use of the services for the learning disabled?		
Does the college or university provide any of the following accommodations: — Test proctors — Extended time on exams — Option for oral exams — Note takers — Tape recorders in classes — Tutorial help specifically for LD students — Textbooks on tape or readers for textbooks		
Does the college or university have equipment that can assist the learning disabled?		
Specifically, does the college or university have any of the following equipment or software programs? — Kurzweil Reader — SoundProof — Dragon Tec		
Does this college provide curriculum modification?		
Does the college provide the option of completing a four-year degree program in five years or longer?		
Does the college or university have an LD support or resource group?		

NOTES:

APPENDIX B:

SCHOOLS WITH EXTENSIVE LD SERVICES

The following colleges and universities are ones that I rate as the top ones in the country for LD students. My criteria are these:

✎ The school has a learning disabilities specialist available to students

✎ The school has a Kurzweil Reader or other adaptive technology available to students

✎ The school has readers to put texts on tape if the book is not available through Recordings for the Blind & Dyslexic.

A If a school meets all of the criteria listed above, then it is a Class A school.

B If a school meets two of the criteria listed above, then it is a Class B school.

C If a school meets one of the criteria listed above, then it is a Class C school.

**A$** If a school meets all of the criteria listed above, but there are extra costs involved, then it is a Class A$ school.

Arizona

 A Arizona State University
Phyllis Jones, Disabled Students
   Resources
Tempe, AZ 85287
602/965-1234

 B University of Arizona
Diane C. Perreira, Strategic Alternate
   Learning Techniques
Tucson, AZ 85721
520/621-1242

California

 B California Polytechnical State University
(also has LD newsletter)
William Bailey, Director, Disability
   Resource Center
San Luis Obispo, CA 93407
805/756-1395

 A San Francisco State University
Joan Kilbourne, Disabled Resource
   Center
San Diego, CA 92182
619/338-2472

California (continued)

 Sonoma State University
Bill Clopton, Disability Resources Center
Rohnert Park, CA 94928
707/664-2677

 Stanford University
Patricia Fleck, Disability Resource
   Center
Stanford, CA 94305
650/723-1066

 University of California (Berkeley)
Helen Beck, Disabled Students Program
Berkeley, CA 94720
510/642-0518

 University of the Pacific
Howard Houck, Office of Learning
   Disability Support
Stockton, CA 95211
209/946-2458

Connecticut

 University of Connecticut
Donna M. Korbell, University Program
   for LD Students
Storrs, CT 06269-4174
860/486-2020

B University of Hartford
Marcia Orcutt, Learning Plus
West Hartford, CT 06117
860/768-4100 X-4522

District of Columbia

 The George Washington University
Christy Willis, Disabled Student Services
Washington, DC 20052
202/994-8250

Florida

B Florida Atlantic University
Miriam Firpo-Lopez, Director
Office for Students with Disabilities
(OSD)
Boca Raton, FL 33431-0991
561-297-3880

 University of Florida
Rick Nelson, Services for Students with
   Disabilities
Gainesville, FL 32611
352/392-1261

Georgia

AS University of Georgia
Sally Scott, Learning Disabilities Center
Athens, GA 30602
706/542-8719

Illinois

B DePaul University
Karen D. Wold, Director
Productive Learning Strategies (PLUS Program)
Chicago, IL 60604
312/362-6897

B Kendall College
Michelle Sinka, Freshman Program
Evanston, IL 60201
847/866-1300 X-1387

B National-Louis University
Carol Eckerman
Services for Students with Special Needs
Evanston, IL 60201
847/475-1100 X02056

C Northern Illinois University
Linda Sorge
Center for Access-Ability Resources (CAAR)
DeKalb, IL 60115
815/753-1303

AS Southern Illinois University
Sally DeDecker
Disability Support Services & Achieve Program
Carbondale, IL 62901
618/453-5738

Indiana

 B Anderson University
Rinda Vogelgesang, Office for Disabled Student Services
Anderson, IN 46012
800/428-6414 or 765/641-4226

C Ball State University
Richard Harris, Disabled Student Development
Muncie, IN 47306
765/285-5293

Indiana *(continued)*

 Purdue University
Jim Johnson, Adaptive Program (AP)
West Lafayette, IN 47907
765/494-1247

 University of Indianapolis
Deborah Spinney, B.U.I.L.D.
Indianapolis, IN 46227
800/232-8634 or 317/788-3536

Iowa

 Loras College
Dianne Gibson, Learning Disabiilties
    Program
Dubuque, IA 52001
800/245-6727 or 319/588-7223

 University of Iowa
Mary Richard, Student Disability
    Services
Iowa City, IA 52242
319/335-1462

Kansas

 Kansas State University
Andrea Blair, Disabled Student Services
Manhattan, KS 66506
785/532-6441

Maine

 Unity College
James Horan, Student Support Services
Unity, ME 04988
207/948-3131

 University of New England
Maura O'Conner, Individual Learning
    Program (ILP)
Biddeford, ME 04005
207/283-0171 X-2561

Maryland

Towson State University
Veronica Uhland, Disability Support
    Services
Towson, MD 21252-0001
410/830-3475

University of Maryland
Peggy Hayeslip, Disability Support
    Services
College Park, MD 20742-8111
301/314-9969

Massachusetts

A$ American International College
Mary Saltus
Supportive Learning Services for
Learning Disabled Students
Springfield, MA 01109
413/737-6420

A$ Boston University
Carrie Lewis, Learning Disabilities
  Support Services
Boston, MA 02215
617/353-3658

B Clark University
Alan Bier, Disability Service
Worcester, MA 01610
508/793-7468

A$ Curry College
Lisa Ijiri, Director,
Program for Advancement for Learning
(PAL)
Milton, MA 02186
617/333-2120 X-2247

A$ Mount Ida College
Jill Mehler, Learning Opportunities
  Program
Newton Centre, MA 02159
617/928-4648

A$ Northeastern University
Beth Rodgers-Kay, Disability Resource
  Center
Boston, MA 02115
617/337-2675

Missouri

C Washington University
Fran Lang, Disability Resource Center
St. Louis, MO 63130-4899
314/935-8516

A$ Westminster College
Hank F. Ottinger, Learning Disabilities
  Program
Fulton, MO 65251
573/592-5304

Minnesota

A University of Minnesota
Bobbi Cordano, Disability services
Minneapolis, MN 55455-0213
612/624-4120

New Hampshire

 Notre Dame College
Jane O-Neil, Learning Enrichment Center
Manchester, NH 03104-2299
603/669-4294

New Jersey

 Fairleigh Dickinson University
Mary Farrell, Regional Center for College
   Students with Learning Disabilities
Rutherford, NJ 07666-1966
201/692-2087

New York

 Adelphi University
Susan Spencer, Learning Disabled
   College Students
Garden City, NY 11530
516/877-4710

Cornell University
Disability Services, Office of Equal
   Opportunity
Ithaca, NY 14853
607/255-3976

Hofstra University
Ignacio Gotz, Program for Academic
   Learning Skills (PALS)
Hemstead, NY 11549
516/463-5841

Iona College
Madeline Packerman, College
   Assistance Program (CAP)
New Rochelle, NY 10801
914/633-2582

Long Island University-C. W. Post College
Carol Rundlett, Academic Resource
   Center (ARC)
Brookville, NY 11548
516/299-2937

Marist College
Linda Cooper
Office of Special Services, Learning
Disabilities Program
Poughkeepsie, NY 12601-1387
914/575-3274

A Rochester Institute of Technology
Carla Katz, Learning Support Services
Rochester, NY 14623
716/475-5296

B St. Lawrence University
John Meagher, Office of Special Needs
Canton, NY 13617
315/229-5104

A$ St. Thomas Aquinas College
Erica Warren, The "STAC" Exchange
Sparkill, NY 10976
914/398-4230

A Syracuse University
Bethany Heaton Crawford, Learning
  Disability Services
Syracuse, NY 13244
315/443-3976

North Carolina

C Appalachian State University
Arlene Lundquist, Learning Disability
  Program
Boone, NC 28608
704/262-2291

C East Carolina University
C. C. Rowe, Department for Disability
  Support
Greenville, NC 27858-4353
252/328-6799

B Western Carolina University
Carol Mellon, Disability Student Services
Cullowhee, NC 28723
828/227-7234

A$ Wingate College
Linda Stedje-Larson, Specific Learning
  Disabilities
Wingate, NC 28174-0157
704/233-8269

Ohio

A$ Muskingum College
Amy Butts, PLUS Program
New Concord, OH 43762
740/826-8137

C University of Cincinnati
Debra Merchant, Disability Services
Cincinnati, OH 45221-009
513/556-6823

Oklahoma

 Oklahoma State University
Debra Swoboda, Student Disability
    Services
Stillwater, OK 74078
405/744-7116

Pennsylvania

 College Misericordia
Joseph Rogan, Alternative Learners
    Project
Dallas, PA 18612
717/674-6347

 East Stroudsburg University of
Pennsylvania
Edith F. Miller, Disability Services
East Stroudsburg, PA 18301-2999
570/422-3825

 Edinboro Univerity of Pennsylvania
Kathleen Strosser, Office for Students
    with Disabilities (OSD)
Edinboro, PA 16444
814/732-2462

 Mercyhurst College
Tina King, Program for Students with
    Learning Differences
Erie, PA 16546
814/824-2450

 Pennsylvania State University
Marianne Karwacki, Learning Disabilities
    Support Services
University Park, PA 16802-3000
814/863-2291

Tennessee

 University of Tennessee at Chattanooga
Debra Anderson, College Access
    Program (CAP)
Chattanooga, TN 37403
423/755-4006

Texas

 University of North Texas
Dee Wilson, Office of Disability
   Accommodations
Denton, TX 76203
940/565-4323

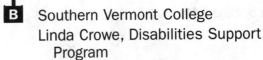 Texas A&M University
Anne Reber, Students with Disabilities
College Station, TX 77843-1265
409/845-1637

 Southwestern Texas State University
Tina Schultz, Office of Disability services
   (ODS)
San Marcos, TX 78666
512/245-3451

Vermont

 Norwich University
Paula A. Gills, Learning Support Center
   (LSC)
Northfield, VT 05663
802/485-2130

 Southern Vermont College
Linda Crowe, Disabilities Support
   Program
Bennington, VT 05201
802/442-6360

Virginia

 University of Virginia
Valerie Schoolcraft
Learning Needs & Evaluation Center
(LNEC)
Charlottesville, VA 22906
804/243-5180

Virginia Intermont College
Barbara Holbrook, Student Support
   Services
Bristol, VA 24201-4298
540/669-6101

West Virginia

 Marshall University
Lynne Weston
Higher Education for Learning Problems
(HELP)
Huntington, WV 25755
304/696-6316

Wisconsin

 University of Wisconsin (Eau-Clair)
Joseph C. Hisrich
Services for Students with Disabilities
(SSD)
Eau Claire, WI 54701
715/836-5415

 University of Wisconsin (LaCrosse)
June Reihert, Disability Resource
  Services
LaCrosse, WI 54601-3742
608/785-6900

USEFUL ORGANIZATIONS AND RESOURCES

ORGANIZATIONS THAT PROVIDE SERVICES AND PRODUCTS FOR THE LEARNING DISABLED

Council for Learning Disabilities (CLD)

P. O. Box 40303
Overland Park, KS 62204
913/492-8755

ERIC Clearinghouse on Adult, Career, and Vocational Education

A clearinghouse with 24-hour voice mail service providing information, bibliographies, and publications on learning disabilities. It does not answer specific questions.

Center for Employment, Education & Training
College of Education
The Ohio State University
1900 Kenny Road
Columbus, OH 43210-1090
614/292-7069 or 800/848-4815 X–2-7069
Fax: 614/292-1260
E-mail: ericacve@postbox.acs.ohio_state.educ

Higher Education and Adult Training for People with Handicaps (HEATH)

One Dupont Circle, Suite 800
Washington, DC 20036
202/939-9320 or 800/544-3284

International Dyslexia Association

Chester Building
8600 LaSalle Road, Suite 382
Baltimore, MD 21286-2044
410/296-0232 or 800/222-3123
e-mail: info@interdys.org

Job Accommodation Network (JAN)

JAN provides disability-specific information on equipment and accommodations for the work place as well as a free consulting service.

West Virginia University
P. O. Box 6080
Morgantown, SV 26506-6080
800/526-7324
Fax: 304/293-5407
e-mail: jan@jan.ic.di.wvu.edu

National Center for Law and Learning Disabilities (NCLLD)

NCLLD is a non-profit education and advocacy organization providing legal information and resources for the learning disabled.

P. O. Box 368
Cabin John, MD 20818
301/469-8308

NARIC (National Rehabilitation Information Center)

8455 Colesville Road, Suite 935
Silver Spring, MD 20910-3319
800/346-2742

National Center for Learning Disabilities (NCLD)

381 Park Avenue South, Suite 1402
New York, NY 10016
212/545-7510 or 888/575-7373
Fax: 212/545-9665

Video Tapes

A Leader's Guide for Youth with Learning Disabilities

A ten-minute film that shows group leaders how to include people with learning disabilities into programs using Boy Scouts as examples. Commentary by Dr. Larry Silver.

Learning Disabilities Association of American (LDA)
4156 Library Road
Pittsburgh, PA 15234-1349
412/341-1515 or 412/341-8077
Fax: 412/344-6224
Website: www.ldanatl.org

Internet Resources

EASI (Equal Access to Software and Information)

Although this site is dedicated to professionals interested in access to math and science, others may find useful information on publications, technology, and internet resources for students with disabilities.

www.rit.edu/~easi

FinAid Page

The Smart Student Guide to Financial Aid includes information on scholarships and fellowships for students with disabilities.

www.finaid.org/documents/heath

LDOnline

This site is for anyone interested in learning disabilities. It includes articles and information as well as a celebrity quiz, artwork and a bulletin board with announcements and job postings.

www.ldonline.org/

Technology Access Center of Tucson, Inc.

This e-mail site has information on assistive technology.

tactaz@aol.com

WLDADD (Women and Learning Disabilities and ADHD)

Professionals and others interested in adult women and learning disabilities, especially those with learning differences themselves, are welcome to this listserv.

To subscribe, send the following command in the body of mail to Listserv@home.ease.lsoft.com: Subscribe WLDADD yourfirstname yourlastname." Contact the list owner for more information.

ABOUT THE AUTHOR

Joy Cobb currently works as a site manager for MAXIMUS Inc. As a licensed vocational rehabilitation counselor and rehabilitation provider, Joy manages a project funded by the Social Security Administration in which enhanced vocational and psychological services are provided to SSI recipient youth. As a private consultant, Ms. Cobb presents seminars and workshops on employment issues related to the disabled in the workplace. She also provides academic and vocational counseling, consulting, and accommodation assessments for the disabled in transition. Since January of 1995, Ms. Cobb has served as the president of LEAD (Learning and Employment for Adult Dyslexics), an adult resource and support group for adults with learning disabilities.

Joy Cobb graduated from The George Washington University (GWU) in Washington, DC with a BA in Psychology in 1992 and was also the recipient of the GWU Leadership Award. She received her MA from GWU in 1995 in Education and Human Development with a specialty in Vocational Rehabilitation Counseling, and was selected to be the GWU student commencement speaker.

Ms. Cobb has been a featured speaker for disabled students at GWU as part of campus community outreach and awareness. She has also made presentations for the Washington-Area Orton Dyslexia Society and for LEAD. Ms. Cobb has been a featured speaker for disabled students at GWU as part of campus and learning disabled students to U.S. Department of Defense teachers; to GWU career counseling classes, school counseling classes and special education classes; and to local high schools.

In 1993, Ms Cobb co-founded the Professionals with Disabilities Resource Network, a clearinghouse for resources, organizations, contacts, and equipment useful for learning disabled professionals.

In addition, she is an "on-call" counselor on the psychiatric unit at Georgetown University Hospital. As a volunteer for the Falls Church Jaycees, she also assists in organizing community outreach projects for the disadvantaged. As Community Development Vice President (1993–94), she has organized AIDS education workshops and training and took second place in the SPEAK-UP competition in the Virginia state competition in 1993.

Ms. Cobb is a member of Chi Sigma Iota, the national counseling honor society and was selected for the 1995 peer presentations program. Other professional affiliations are the American Counseling Association (ACA), Association for Assessment in Counseling (AAC), National Association for Rehabilitation Counselors (NARC), American Rehabilitation Counseling Association (ARCA), and the Learning Disabilities Association (LDA).

Ms. Cobb is available to provide presentations, workshops, seminars, and motivational speeches to students by contacting her at the following address:

Learning How to Learn
147 North French Street
Alexandria, VA 22304
Telephone: (703) 823-8348
Email: seacob@CWIX.com
Fax: (703) 823-8349

1993